South to North

A Rocky Road to Faith

Dear Trey,
You asked me once
about how I came
to faith.. now you
know!
With blessings
Nigel & Jane pp

-Nigel Perrott -

Cover design by Fiona Smith

Printed by Book Printing UK www.bookprintinguk.com
Remus House, Coltsfoot Drive, Peterborough, PE2 9BF

Printed in Great Britain

ISBN: 978-03691705-0

Acknowledgements

With Grateful thanks to Eric Bridgstock, for helping me to get our story down on paper and dealing with my many odd words.

Anita, who we now know as a dear friend and whose home became ours as I finished this book.

Ian & Audrey whose prayer and companionship has been with us from the start of the journey.

The Methodist Diaconal Order for unending prayer and food for the journey ahead.

Fiona Smith for translating Jane's dream into the picture that appears on the cover of this book.

Quotations

Lewis and Cordeiro, with Bird, Culture Shift, Published by Jossey-Bass, (2005)

Dedicated to our precious friends Andy & Pricilla

Without them, and Jesus, there would be
no story to tell.

Contents

Preface

The following pages contain a story, the story of my life married to Jane and a life that involves Jesus at its heart. I do hope it will make people smile, cry, and everything else in between.

Jane and I decided some time ago that our journey should be documented. Over the years we have kept many prayer letters and journals, and the account that follows has used those memories to complete a picture of how Jane and I grew on our journey with Jesus. A journey that took us from the South of England on a long road to the North. That journey was often like climbing a mountain, which I did in North Africa.

There was a time in recent memory when I had no time for faith, the church, and certainly not Christians. The only time Jane mentioned God was when she stubbed her toe on the side of the bed. We both know what life is like without the knowledge of Jesus. The knowledge we've both discovered has changed our entire lives.

I do hope that our story helps to encourage readers, but I also want to show how the church we are now a part of has sometimes given mixed messages. As our story progressed there were so many occasions, when we felt disillusioned.

We know that Christianity began with a relationship, however, we both found over the years that this relationship can become transactional, "I will show you what God's love is, and then you can become like me". You can get up on a Sunday morning, attend my church, and adhere to all the unwritten rules that will no doubt be given to you. This may well include things such as, what kettle to use, who oversees the notice board and of course the most important thing of all, where you are allowed to sit!

The way in which Jane and I lived out our newfound faith was often very different from the norm, and this caused difficulties along the way. We have discovered that the church can be complicated and often not understood by those hearing the message. I am not just talking about words, terminology and symbols, though they were certainly alien to us for a long time! No, it's not just about words but an understanding of who a person is. Let me put it like this: You can live anywhere in the world, but if you don't speak the language, it's going to be difficult. How more beneficial would it be, if you were able to speak the recipient's language too? If I understand their language, sharing Jesus should be easier, right?

The journey of faith that Jane and I found did not start in church, we didn't get an invitation to a course, to read a book, or a flyer, not that these are wrong. My own early experiences of church had a huge negative impact on my life. By the time I reached middle age, church and faith were a forgotten memory, I mistrusted the church and everything that went with it. When God finally had enough of our failures, it was not an invite to church that would change things. It started with a conversation, a conversation that was all about me and Jane. Someone took the time to understand us, and from there, share something of Jesus with us. That relationship gained the right to speak into our lives and change things for the better. In a simplistic way, we discovered who we were, what made us tick and then saw how this could look to someone else. From there we have tried to use our life experiences to help others see a different outcome from one the world might give them. The good news of Jesus is available to all, and we hope that along the way we can continue to share that good news in different and exciting ways. When we as the church get this right, and we often do, the results are amazing.

I think I will leave it to you, the reader, to decide if we got it right! If nothing else, our story is about a Jesus who has walked with us, blessed us and has given us a life, a life full of joy, and although sadness, and even some catastrophe has been present, we were able to get through it.

The bible tells me:

"Do not conform any longer to the pattern of this world, but be transformed by the renewing of your minds, then you will be able to test and approve what God's will is, his good, pleasing and perfect will"
Romans 12:2- New International Version

*What you are about to read is a true story, it involves real people and real places. To protect identities, I have chosen to change names, with their permission, and leave out the name of the towns we moved from and to.

Chapter 1 - The Early Years

As I sat in my seat, arms folded, I gazed around the hall. The gym equipment neatly folded away against the walls, a rather tatty piano perched against one of the walls, walls that clearly need a new coat of paint. Pictures adorned them; I am sure cheery children would have painted them in weeks gone by. I was sat on a rather uncomfortable hard plastic chair that had been eagerly placed there by a team of volunteers who had clearly been there for some time before we arrived. Looking to the front I saw two large black speakers on what looked like rather dodgy stands perched either side of a makeshift stage. A band made up of a group of quite scruffy young people were playing something, I wasn't too sure what. Whatever it was nobody really seemed to take notice. People continued to stream into the school hall. I saw quite a lot of hugs, and people greeting each other with what I could only describe as overexcited hysteria. I had felt uncomfortable when I arrived, now I was feeling despair. I looked at the exit longingly, in this crowd, I could easily just walk out without being noticed. I turned to look at Jane, surely by now she would be feeling the same and we could sneak out. My heart sank as I turned to see Jane smiling and clearly enjoying the atmosphere of total chaos. Jane is the definition of an extrovert, I am not.

Though not in this school hall, I had been here before. In years gone by, I had experienced what I now know to be a "Charismatic Church", or "Happy Clappy" as it is more affectionately known, I had attended a formal church too, as a child when at boarding school. Now in my thirties, those times just made me wretch. So here I am, once again, sat in a row with a bunch of what I can only describe as aging hippies, waiting for a concert to start. To make matters worse, the man who had invited us to this mayhem was nowhere to be seen. I glanced around, trying not to make eye contact with anyone. I certainly didn't need a hug or get into a big conversation about Jesus with a total stranger. My uneasiness turned to embarrassment, and I was just willing the whole debacle to be over. Christians were to me, the epitome of a hypocrite, a total nonsense that needed to be avoided in the same way you might hide when the Jehovah Witnesses knock at your door.

Nobody seemed to notice the guy with a bald head walk towards the stage with a large microphone in his hand. As his voice began to speak, it was hardly audible over the continuing racket of excited voices and the noise from the electric guitar behind him.

Little did I know, that in the moments that would follow, my life would never be the same.

How we arrived at this place, has always been a large part of our story. The day that a guy arrived in our café and began to make friends with Jane, is, and will always be a source of amusement, to us and to him.

Martin was a local businessman; he had an office just a few steps away from our café. The Palette Café was located inside an Arts Centre in the heart of the Old Town. We had taken over the lease a few months before and business was okay, but not exactly booming. Though Jane and I had both been caterers, we had probably taken on more than we could chew - sorry about the pun!

Martin was in marketing and his advice was needed, in more ways than one. He had a smile and a way about him that was pleasant and welcoming. Jane took a shine to him straight away. A tall man, well-dressed but casual. His striking white hair and nice shoes were something Jane approved of. I, on the other hand, was a little more suspicious - there was something about his personality that struck me. He was a listener and his quiet demeanour quite comforting. "I really like him; he is just nice and really wants to help" Jane announced one morning.

That was the day he ordered his usual bacon sandwich and coffee. That was the day I understood who he was. "Yes", I said, "he's a Christian". In that moment, I made up my mind that he was not to be trusted. Christians really had only one thing on their minds, and it certainly was not our best interests. I was pleasant and even started to engage with some of his Christian musings. I was not unfamiliar with Christians, I had had my experiences in the past, experiences I certainly did not want to repeat. At this point in my life, Jane was completely unaware that I had been in a church, professed Jesus as my Lord, and even been a part of a church youth group. That experience had led me to a point that all Christians were lunatics, and I was never going to darken the doorway of another church. No, best keep him at arm's length, make him a bacon sandwich and treat him like any other customer.

One evening back at our little house, Jane was quietly making the tea and chatting about the day. Saucepan in hand, and smiling, Jane quite enthusiastically announced, "We have been invited to lunch". "That's nice", I replied, not really taking that much notice. I am not really a very social person and am more than happy in my own space.

"Who?" I asked. "Martin, he said he has an open house after church on a Sunday". In that moment my heart sank, I knew it, he would weasel himself into my life and before I knew it, I would be stuck in a pew reciting total rubbish from some kind of prayer book.

"You have to be kidding" I said, quite angrily. "There is no way I want to go to church". Jane was puzzled, and I think quite shocked at my outburst. Not that outbursts were uncommon in our house. It didn't take much to send me off into a rage, especially if I had had too much to drink. By this time in my life, I had things more under control, the anger had diminished from my days when alcohol had taken a hold. I was more settled, and my past life of alcohol and soft drugs were behind me. Sadly, it didn't take much for that inner anger to show itself.

"He didn't say church", she shouted. Maybe not, I replied, "but you wait and see".

The idea of going to a church and pretending that the world was lovely just fuelled my inner, hidden anger. This was to be made all the worse by the next statement from Jane's lips. "Just because you don't like Christians doesn't mean I can't, I am Christian", she shouted at me. I laughed, "You are not a Christian!" "I am" she replied", getting angrier herself, "I was christened". My sarcastic laughter grew louder, "Just because you were christened as a baby does not make you a Christian", and at this point I became aggressive, that it what it took to make my point. It was clear that an argument was not going to convince Jane that this was a bad idea. We went through into the lounge and began to eat. "Listen", I said, more softly, realising that I needed to calm down. "To be a Christian means that you have decided to follow Jesus, you make a commitment to change". I continued to talk about what was understood about how people become Christians. "They believe that the only way to know God is through Jesus, it's not just about being a good person", I tried to speak softly, not being too overbearing. I thought if I used some logic, Jane would understand, and we could put this behind us. I talked through all I knew, telling Jane about my own past in church, and the Jesus that people talked about.

To my horror, Jane began to cry. "I want to know this Jesus" What I had thought would put Jane off, had the opposite effect. "I want to go to church" When Jane made up her mind that was it, nothing I said or did was going to change it.

“We will go to church and go back to lunch, you can stay at home if you like, but I am going”. Not wanting a full-blown argument, I quietly gave in. Arguments in our house were frequent, and my stepdaughter sadly witnessed many of them. Not today, I thought.

Chapter 2 – Just me

Having now given in and knowing that this weekend I would once again be heading off to church, my mind travelled back to my childhood. I was one of four, the youngest in fact. Six years from my closest sibling and ten years from the eldest.

My childhood was complicated and could probably fuel another book. My parents worked hard, probably too hard. There was no lack of love, and I was brought up well. I can't remember going to church as a small child, we certainly didn't go as a family, and we didn't do much as a family full stop.

My middle sister on the other hand was a Christian, how she got there is her own story. I do remember her coming home from youth group and telling me stories.

When I was a little older, I went to boarding school. How I ended up there is just another reminder to me that my parents worked hard.

I hated boarding school. I was bullied, bullied by other kids, and bullied by the teachers. It is a time I try and block out; it brings only painful memories.

The respite from this time was always the trips to Bristol to stay with my sister in the holidays. She lived a house full of other girls, all nurses and all quite mad. They were all Christians, full of life and full of fun. My first visit to their church was a shock. Nothing like the kind of church I was forced to go to while at school.

Church at school was compulsory. Each Sunday morning, I would have to dress in my sports jacket, smart shirt, flannel trousers, and a tie. It was as uncomfortable as the service itself in the old church we had to attend. A typical old church with an arched gate, leading through a yard of crumbling gravestones and overgrown grass. We were always greeted by a band of what felt like angry old women. Their hard stares of distain always focused on this group of Grammar School boys arriving for their weekly torture. "Remember boys, no talking, no fidgeting - Mr Johnson, will be hearing if you misbehave", It was the same each week, just repeated by different dragons.

I have to say we always talked, always fidgeted and always had the eyes of older ladies fixed on us. Mr Johnson often heard of our behaviour, good or bad, and the consequence of which was always a visit to his study.

The hour-long service of sung Eucharist always felt like a week. It was always a mystery and though we attended the compulsory classes to fully understand what we were doing; the point of this ritual was still completely alien to us.

One summer, I told my mother about this awful experience. Her response really surprised me. "Well, you could go to the Methodist Church if you like, your grandmother was a Methodist. I went to the chapel as a child". I was quite surprised at her response, the thought of my mum being in a church had never occurred to me.

My mum duly contacted the school, and, on my return, my house master summoned me to his study. With no greeting, which was not unusual, he announced, "Perrott", your mother has informed us that you are Methodist", you didn't tell us, why not? "I didn't know Sir", I was trembling, that's what you did when you had been summoned to his rather dark and gloomy room.

"We like to accommodate different religions here, so you will attend The Methodist Church from this Sunday".

I will always remember his rather pompous kindness! I was also quite surprised that my mother had some kind of other religion. I left his office feeling slightly relieved that, for once, this meeting was less stressful, and less painful for that matter, than those I had previously had in his oak-walled study.

Sunday morning duly arrived and as the other boys were sent off to church, I sat in the common room. A large room with tatty armchairs, with old smelly T-shirts and sport equipment strewn around the floor. A large billiards table in the centre, the green baize had long since given up and the slate was visible through the many tears. I had an hour or so before I needed to head off to my "other religion" service. There was an unusual sense of peace in the air, I had the place to myself, and I enjoyed it. Time passed and the peace was about to be shattered, as the other boys would now be on their way back. I had already been victimised for not going to the traditional church and the idea that I could in some way get out of going had not gone down well. I decided to get out before they arrived.

As I left the school grounds and walked along the road, leaving the foreboding Victorian building behind me, I felt a relief. I was free for at least a couple of hours. The Methodist Church was a short walk from the school, so I decided to take the long way. I ducked down a side path and found myself walking along the canal. It was a cold but bright morning, and the freedom and brisk autumn air filled my lungs. I sat on a bench next to the calm water. The odd dog walker bustling through, cyclists and old people just enjoying this quiet morning. Sitting on a bench, dressed in my "church clothes", probably looked rather odd, but nobody seemed to take much notice. Time ticked by and I felt no inclination to get to the church. In that moment, a thought came to me, "who would know?" I smiled and my plan was complete.

From that Sunday on, my Sunday routine was complete. Sit around the common room, head off to "church" and spend the time at the canal. I had thought correctly, nobody challenged me and, as far as I was concerned, free to do what I wanted for a couple of hours each Sunday morning. Though I was often bullied for going to a weird church, the taunts were worth the freedom of being somewhere else, just for a while at least.

My little walks on the canal lasted for several weeks. It, however, was not to last.

Matron, or Maggie as we knew her, looked after the boarders. A short but well-built lady, with grey hair always held in a neat bun. More Grandma than mum. She would ensure our dorms were tidy, that we washed, and generally did what we were told when we were in the boarding house. Her deep broad Yorkshire accent would boom out to us in the morning, that and a large bell that she would wave enthusiastically, to ensure we heard "Cum on boys, time for break-fust" Looking back she was a lovely old soul, who really cared about us. It was Maggie who would put an end to my little Sunday walks.

One evening as I was ironing my shirts, something we had to do under Maggie's instruction. "So, how are you finding the Methodist Church?"

I shrugged my shoulders, "its ok", I replied, still trying to hide my real thoughts. "Mr Johnson tells me that you have been attending since the start of term". "Yes, I replied", realising that something was going horribly wrong. "I have been a member of the church for over 40 years, and I have never seen you", my face flushed, my ruse was over in the most embarrassing way, and when Mr Johnson found out, I would be in a whole heap of trouble.

The following Sunday, Maggie would meet me and take me along to the church. She never did tell my housemaster; I think she really was a kind old soul.

I attended the church for the remainder of my school years, and gradually felt more at home and the more informal services certainly were a relief from the incense and candles I had experienced in the other church. I always enjoyed the informal talks the preacher would give, though much of it did go over my head.

By the time I went along to my sister's church in Bristol my idea of church was already tainted. Church was something I was forced to do, and not something I ever wanted, or needed. It was completely out of touch with me. Where was this Jesus, when I was being bullied and shouted at?

"Pip 'n' Jay" - St Philip and Jacob, its full name - would be a whole new level of amazement. From the outside, it was not dissimilar to the old church back at school. An old Victorian hunk of stone set in a graveyard. Why would anyone want to go into a building that was surrounded by dead bodies?

There were no smartly dressed people here, more T-shirt and shorts than jacket and tie. As I approached the church with my sister and her friends, we were greeted with smiles. I was amazed at how many people were pouring into this building on a Sunday night. As I walked through the large wooden doors, the rows and rows of pews were filled with people, mostly young, not much older than me.

There was a band, and I was shocked that a drum kit could be allowed in such a place. The service began, the band played and after some time of singing songs we were asked to sit.

This was a church I had never seen before, and the informal feeling made me feel at home. The vicar, a large middle-aged man, dressed all in black, the odd food stain on his jacket and the typical white collar, began to speak. I had seen him outside before the service, smoking a large cigar and puffing smoke joyfully into the air. This was something I had definitely not seen before. As he spoke, the words went over my head, I've no idea what was being said, it could have been in French. There was a quiet hush as people seemed to be hanging on each word. As he ended, he turned and pointed at a large red curtain that hung from the roof and covered the whole of the front of the church. "If you want to know more about Jesus, come down to the front and go behind the curtain" I was completely amazed as people began walking down to the front of the church and going behind the curtain. What was this? Was there some kind of other realm in there, was there an angel, or even Jesus himself waiting to bring people to some other plane? I watched in amazement, and curiosity took over. I had no intention of meeting Jesus but what was going on intrigued me. My feet took over and I followed others, so, I too, could get to see what was going on. I walked at quite a pace, as I approached the curtain an excitement came over me, what was behind this strange curtain. As I brushed the curtain aside, I found myself, not in another dimension but in the front of the church. Little huddles of people standing around while someone held their hands over them, muttering and chatting with their eyes tightly closed. "Is this it?" I thought. All this anticipation, to see a group of strange people hanging around the front of a draughty old church with their hands in the air. It was at that point I was approached, "Hi, I am John, you're Marion's brother, aren't you?" Yes, I replied with rather a stutter, I had no idea what I was doing there. John didn't hold his hands above me, thankfully. "So, what do you want to know about Jesus?" I had no idea what to say, still in shock from the disappointment of the curtain. "I don't really", I stuttered, I don't want to know anything, I just wanted to know what was going on behind the curtain". John roared with laughter; he was a big man but had a gentle smile. John chatted with me, and I shared with him how I felt about school. I felt safe with him and wanted to tell someone about how I felt. He listened to me. No prayers or words of wisdom, he just listened.

John would continue to write to me when I was at school, sending the odd bible verse in for good measure. By the time I had left school, I lost touch with John. I remember fondly the times we met when I wasn't at school and all the chats we had.

Years went by and the time came when I would finally be released from the torment of school. No rules to follow, no church on Sundays, freedom to do what I wanted to do, when I wanted to do it.

This new freedom would only lead to more sadness, for me, and for my mum and dad. It took several years and a few convictions for petty offences before I would truly get over those awful days of school. Without really knowing, I had grown an inner anger and resentment of life. I needed to find something that could replace this inner hurt. My church attendance became a distant memory, and a bottle of Newcastle Brown took the place of any communion wine I had had while at school. Alcohol would prove to be the easiest replacement for most of my hidden feelings.

After several failed attempts at finding a job or career that suited, I ended up in the hotel trade. I trained as a manager and my life became better. That is when I met Lorna.

Lorna was new, just like me. We had started at the same time in a brand-new hotel. She was about my age, mid-twenties, and had started as a receptionist. Lorna had a welcoming personality, and I was immediately attracted to her smile. I set about asking her on a date. I did my best over the coming weeks, and though always very polite, she was clearly not interested in going anywhere with me. That didn't put me off and I tried several ways to coax her. After a few weeks of trying, I thought I would give it one more try before giving up.

"There's a band playing in town at the weekend, would you like to go?" almost knowing her answer before she opened her mouth to reply. She smiled, she always smiled, “You are persistent, I’ll give you that”, almost laughing at me. “Well, what do you think”?

I tell you what, I will come with you, on one condition” I had almost given up on Lorna, so conditions seemed okay to me. “Your wish is my command I replied”.

Her condition would almost cause me to fall over. “If you come to church with me on Sunday night, I’ll come and see that band”.

I was surprised that this lovely girl would have anything to do with church, but the offer couldn’t be refused. Besides, I knew what church was about, I could handle an hour of church to spend time with Lorna. It had been a long time since I had sat in a pew and the thought didn’t fill me with joy. “Okay, you’re on, I’ll come”. Lorna smiled, she didn’t seem to be that surprised that I had said yes, and this felt rather suspicious to me.

Sunday evening duly arrived; I met Lorna outside the local “Baptist” church. I was all leather jacket and boots in those days but decided a more formal but casual approach was needed for this occasion. Smart shirt and trousers would make the right impression. To my shock, Lorna arrived wearing a tatty denim jacket and jeans. Perhaps Lorna was really a rebellious and reluctant church goer after all. She just needed someone to come along and make her feel better. The church was very modern, probably ten or so years old. A large open foyer greeted me as I walked in. It struck me that everyone was a similar age, and the atmosphere was informal. As I glanced around, most of the people were dressed in jeans and T-shirts. A throwback to Pip 'n' Jay, I thought. "I can do this," I said to myself.

Lorna ushered me into the main church, a big space with soft chairs and a carpeted floor, not a pew in sight. I was quietly impressed how comfy the whole place looked. Plenty of young people and quite an informal atmosphere. As I took my seat, a tall guy, wearing trainers, T-shirt and a big smile, slapped me on my back, "great to see you Nige". I was a little taken aback, how does this guy know me? I turned to look at Lorna who was grinning all over her face, "Oh, I told him you were coming tonight" My suspicions started to rise, "What am I doing here?"

The tall guy wandered up to the front of the church and began to speak. "It's great to see you all here tonight. I know that we are looking forward to hearing what Graham is going to share with us".

It was now quiet in the room, he said a prayer and welcomed Graham to thc front. No songs, no hymns, I was slightly relieved and settled into my seat.

Graham smiled as he took the microphone in his hand, sweeping the wire away from his knees as he sat on a chair and began to speak. Graham had clearly seen some sights in his time, his broad Scottish accent began to explain who he was. As he began to talk about his childhood and his school years I began to listen more intently. Bullied at school, going off the rails and getting into trouble with the Police. That was my story! As he progressed through his life story, I realised why Lorna had brought me. By the time he ended his story I was almost in tears. As his story ended, I realised that it was Jesus who had changed this guy's life. That evening, I gave my life to Christ, my first steps as a proper follower of Jesus.

What of Lorna? Lorna and I remained friends, we never went on a proper date, and I often smile when I think about how she got me into church.

I remained in the church for around six months. I had to leave when my job took me to Devon. It was all downhill from there.

I did try to find a new church but had no idea of where to start. My old church hadn't kept in touch, and I ended up going anywhere that said "Church". Some churches just looked like the horror house that I found while at school, others were just odd. I even found myself one evening sat in a circle in someone's front room. I left when I was told I had a demon and needed to be exorcised! I had no idea what that meant and I was certainly not going to stay and find out. Each place I went, I was either ignored or had someone wanting to put their grubby hand on my head. After a year or so, the church was replaced by the pub and my life of church and Jesus were truly left behind. The hidden anger and resentment returned. Who really needs these weirdos anyway?

Chapter 3 – Jane

Years went by, and my career reached new highs and new lows. Working in a hotel brought a social life I enjoyed. I made lots of friends and knew exactly how to have a good time. I was always the life and soul of the party and, at one time, gained the nickname of: "Nige, the world's greatest chicken impersonator".

My world involved two things, work plus alcohol and as the years went by, alcohol certainly started to take first place.

By the time I had reached the Channel Islands, I was firmly in the "work hard", "play hard" regime. I had taken on the role of bar manager in a local cabaret club. I worked six days a week serving drinks to eager tourists who wanted to see a good show. It was mundane and repetitive, but my evenings would always end up in a good drinking time with other local bar owners. My Sundays on the island were very different; it was a day off, and the bars opened early. This meant one thing, I could start early.

It was Monday morning, my head was hurting, my mouth dry, the sun beamed through the window and my eyes squinted in the harsh light. I heard the buzzing of flies and in my disoriented state brushed them off with the sheet I was lying on. As I started to get my bearings, a sense of horror came over me. I looked at the sheet, my bed was damp, I sat up quickly and the horror became more intense. The whole bed was covered in vomit. I had no clue how I had even got into bed, let alone how I had managed to end up in my bed in this state. I got up, staggered to the shower and tried to get myself sorted. The hot water streamed onto my head, which was still pulsating in pain. Getting out of the shower, I grabbed a towel. Once dried, I found my T-shirt and shorts and staggered into the bar. The building had its own accommodation block at the rear of the building. My room was just a few steps to the bar entrance. I walked across the hallway and hobbled into the bar; I found the kettle and did my best to try and make a drink. Once made, I took my black coffee over to the bar and generously poured Jack Daniels into the cup. This I had found was the best cure for a hangover. My hands were shaking, and I knew that last night must have been a particularly good night. I needed fresh air and some sun on my face, so I wondered out. I walked out of the fire-door into the car park at the side of the club. It was next to the beach, and I decided to go and sit on the wall to wake up. As I made my way across, I looked in horror, a cold sweat came over me, and I began to shake again. There, parked neatly across two spaces was my car. I always drove into town, would leave my car, and pick it up the next day. Not last night, to my total dismay, I had driven home. As I sat staring at my car, I knew then I had to do something. This ‘play hard’ lifestyle had to end, alcohol had taken over and I had no way to stop it.

It was time to leave, get back to the mainland and cease this crazy alcohol fuelled life.

A few weeks later, I returned to the UK, but it took several months to recover, find a new job and get my life back on track. My sister came to the rescue, and I was able to stay with her until I found a new job.

I never stopped drinking, just slowed things down to a more manageable and enjoyable pace. The odd relapse here and there would lead to another morning of headaches but life in a hotel always led to alcohol at some point and I still enjoyed a good session when the opportunity arose.

After several years working around the country, I ended up in the Cotswolds. A cute little market town with stone houses and a nice market square. I lived in small stone cottage, just a few minutes' walk from my hotel and next door to a nice pub. By this time, alcohol was joined with the use of various pills that would help me get through the long days.

After those long hours I would often frequent my local pub, a quick drink before retiring to bed was always on the cards. On the occasions where I had an afternoon off, the pub was always a welcome relief from the hustle and bustle of hotel life.

One morning I was in my office, and I was joined by one of the cleaners. They were always a happy bunch, and I looked forward to having chat with them as they ran their dusters around the furniture and generally wasted the last hour of their shift.

It was Lynsey's day today. She burst in, big smile on her face, "hey you go to the Black Flag, don't you?", “yes” I replied, rather puzzled, “That’s where Jane works”, “and?” I said, now more puzzled than before. She “fancies you”. I didn’t really know what to say, it was like being back at primary school. I must have blushed in embarrassment, and that sent her into more giggles.” She, and others continued to taunt me about this Jane, and after a few weeks of banter I decided to get this sorted.

The opportunity came one lunch time when I wasn’t working. I would let her down gently, just tell her I wasn’t interested and leave. Jane worked behind the bar, always smiled and was always talking. She had invited me to her birthday party a few weeks before, but the thought of that was just too much. Hopefully, I would not have to apologise too much for not going. I shut my front door and walked the few steps to the pub door. On entering, I realised I was the only customer and that made me feel slightly uneasy. I wandered up to the bar and sat on one of those high stools.

Jane smiled, “Hello Stranger”. I ordered, a pint of Guinness, and thought about how I could say what needed to be said. After twenty minutes of small talk, the weather, am I working hard, and so on, I was starting to pluck up the courage. Jane smiled at me, she had short dark hair, a pink streak to one side. There was something nice about this girl. Maybe today was not the day to say anything. I sipped on my drink and continued to chat. Just then Jane looked at me, smiled, and said, “Are you going to ask me out or what?”, I nearly spat out my drink and, rather than do the whole let down thing, I found the words came out of my mouth without thinking, "Okay, what about Monday Night?" I liked this girl, she was outspoken, forthright and, as I realised, very attractive.

Monday duly arrived, and Jane was an hour late. When she finally arrived at the pub, she was joined by her six-year-old daughter. Emma was having a sleep over at the pub as the owners were good friends of Jane. I dated Jane for a few months and, as the days went by, we became closer and closer. Emma on the other hand would prove to be a little harder to come to terms with.

Time went by, my time with Jane increased, and the 'work hard play hard' life was about to come crashing down. I lost my job at the hotel and needed to find something else. This would lead me to a job 20 miles away and moving was the only option. Jane and I had become very close, and we decided to rent a house together. My new job was incredibly stressful and would often mean working 60-70 hours a week. This often meant staying overnight at the hotel and going home for my day off, when I got one. I really wanted to spend time with Jane, but work was preventing me from having a life. I hadn't realised how my health was suffering, and I was becoming more and more angry. My work was incredibly stressful the long hours and the responsibility was taking its toll.

I woke up one morning in the hotel, knew I had a hectic day ahead, and couldn't face it. Enough was enough, I walked into the reception, placed my keys on the desk and left, never to return. At that stage my mental health had imploded, and I did what I always did when stress raised its ugly head, I drank. With no money, no job, with a partner and child to take care of, life became unbearable. The next six months of my life and things that I did, are not the source of any joy and remind me of the shame. I had to sign on the dole, and felt humiliated every time I walked into the job centre. I had become an angry, out of work alcoholic, and it was Jane and Emma took the brunt. I was never physically violent, but the shouting and throwing of things had become the norm. On a few occasions, Jane would have to take Emma and either stay with her mum or a friend. Each time, I would have to apologise and say I would stop drinking. I took to going to the supermarket to buy my booze, go home through the back door and hide the said drink on top of the kitchen cupboards. I would then go out and come in through the front door, all in the hope that Jane would not know what I had bought. This never worked and my outbursts and anger just returned, time and time again.

I eventually did find a new job, away from hotel life and more normal hours. Through an old friend, I started working for a plant hire company. I went from room allocations and bar work to dumper trucks and Kango hammers. The work was enjoyable and gave me a chance of a better life. The drinking subsided and life became more bearable for all of us. A few years of stability followed, we married and started our own catering business.

We both had always dreamed of having our own café, something to call our own, where we called the shots. This would happen when we saw a little ad in the local paper. A local arts centre was advertising the lease of their café. We jumped at the chance, and to our amazement we got it. Life was on the up.

It was then that Martin arrived.

Chapter 4 - Change & Challenge

The guy with a bald head, Phil, holding a bible in one hand and a mic in the other, was reading. I couldn't hear anything over the din in the room, but slowly voices began to recede, and the words became more audible.

"I have come that they may have life, and life in all its fullness"

In that moment, that was all I could hear, to me, the whole room was silent. Those words echoing around my head. "I have come that they may have life". A sense of peace came over me, along with a sense of realisation. My life was certainly not full, in fact, my heart was empty. I wasn't really that happy - there was something missing in my life. The anger and hurt I had inside had never left me. I was angry with God, very angry. How could this God have brought all those lunatics into my life? How could he have abandoned me? I had not consciously blamed God, but inwardly I was just an irate and irritable man. Then in my head, I heard a voice, "I will do the judging, you just do the living". I sat staring ahead, a stillness came over me that I couldn't understand. For so many years I was angry. Angry with people, angry with myself and angry with God, a God I was determined didn't exist. I hated Christians, I judged them for all their hypocrisy. In this moment of peace, I felt God, yet, even as I thought this, I was still not fully grasping what was happening. In that moment I started to see all the times

God had been there. Through my school years, through Maggie, John, and then Lorna. I started to feel guilty because God had been there all along, I just refused to listen. I had given my life to Jesus all those years ago and he hadn't gone anywhere, I had. This feeling of guilt subsided and in the moments that followed my heart was changing. In what still felt like silence, I said "Okay God, I give in, I need you and I want to serve you full time, whatever it takes". I had no idea why I was saying this, something deep inside was taking over.

I turned to look at Jane, she was crying, she cried a lot in those days. Jane had found Jesus too and her life was about to be transformed. In our own way, we had both encountered a presence, a feeling that we had never felt before. As the service continued, it was all rather a blur, those words echoing in my head "you do the living".

The next day, we returned to the café. The Art Centre had a small, cobbled area as you approached through two large gates. Set in the centre was a large sculpture of two hands held together. The inscription read "The Applause", a reference to the many shows that took place within. I had walked past this on many days, but today something else occurred to me. I turned to Jane and said, "Look, they are praying hands". We laughed and at the same time knew that this seemed to be an encouragement.

We had a new sense of purpose, and everyone would soon know about it. Jane wasted no time in telling everyone that Jesus loved them! Walking into the reception, Jane walked up to the ticket office. May was a young girl who, as well as a performer herself, worked in the office. "Morning May, do you know that Jesus loves you", May was slightly taken a back, "I don't think I have given it much thought", she laughed.

Within days, we were playing Christian music and slowly turning our little space into a "Christian space". We would hold church breakfasts, bible studies and any other church activity we could think of. May and the rest of the team were puzzled at this strange couple who had found Jesus but seemed to go along with the madness that we expressed. I suspect they thought we had lost the plot.

We continued to work hard, and the café became more successful. The downside to the success meant that we, and me in particular, were not seeing the effect this had on Emma. She was still dealing with several issues and though she started to come to church, she was going to struggle. We had worked so hard to make the café a success, before and after becoming Christians, but we had not seen the effect this had on her. I would often brush this off. "She will be fine; she just needs to behave". This became my response to Jane's concerns, and we would still argue about the best way to deal with her problems.

I was ill-prepared to deal with the trauma of what had been in Emma's past, her own dad leaving and our turbulent relationship was going to take its toll. We tried so hard, but it was clearly not enough, and she would run off for days at a time. The police would be called, they would bring her home and the cycle would continue. Emma would have times when she was more settled, and we were all baptised together one Easter Day. We had hoped that this newfound faith Emma was discovering was going to be the answer. It was not.

Sadly, even on the day of our baptism, it transpired that she had been in an inappropriate relationship with one of the boys from Church.
I phoned the Pastor and Martin and asked them to come and see us urgently. Jane was beside herself with worry. "He needs to sort this out, he's the leader". The Pastor arrived along with Martin, and we began explaining what had happened. His response was not what we had expected. He brushed off the event, putting it down to kids being kids. Both Jane and I felt disillusioned with his response. Though Martin had been far more supportive we didn't feel it would be right for us to stay in the church and decided to leave.

Yet again, social services would need to get involved and we felt completely alone in the struggles we were facing. Years of intervention from the authorities, therapy and heartache were to follow. Emma would disappear, and Jane would walk the streets looking for her. On one occasion, Jane was walking through the town looking in the bars and clubs when Emma had disappeared. She prayed, "Lord just bring her out to me". A desperate prayer often said in tears. Just in that moment, Jane glanced through the door of a busy bar, and there she was, standing at the bar surrounded by a group of men. Laughing and joking without a care in the world. There was no way she was going into that bar without some help and managed to find a Policeman. As Emma had already been reported missing, he acted straight away. She was brought home and the next day, she was gone again. The cycle would continue for some time. Finally, after a great deal of intervention, she went into foster care.

This period put a great deal of pressure on our marriage. However, we decided to expand our business and took on a contract at a local sports club. Jane managed this while I was left working in the café. We became distant and both having long days, would hardly speak when we arrived home. Emma was the cause of many arguments and life went downhill very quickly.

I left the café one evening, walking out through the gates, feeling exhausted, mentally and physically. I couldn't go home to another row. I crossed the road from the arts centre and headed to the pub. A real ale pub, the kind of place with low ceilings and a big open fire. The ceiling yellowed with years of cigarette smoke. I liked the peace and quiet, somewhere to get my head together. Having sat in a daze for an hour or so, sipping on my "Old Speckled Hen", I decided another pint wasn't needed and I made my way home. It was dark and cold outside, but I didn't have far to walk back to our apartment in the old town. I reached the front door and climbed the stairs, took a breath and opened the door. Darkness, I fumbled for the light, Jane should have been home by now. I took out my phone, and sent a text, WHERE ARE YOU? A moment passed and the return text arrived. "I'M AT MUMS, GOING TO STAY THE NIGHT". It was not unusual for Jane to go to her mum's. These frequent trips to see "mum" had started to increase. I didn't give it a lot of thought. A few weeks passed and one morning Jane told me she wanted to take a few days away. We had been so distant it was clear we both needed space. "I am going to Brighton for a couple of days" she announced one morning. "I've covered work, I just need space". I nodded and agreed that some time out would not be a bad idea. "How are you getting there?", "I am going to take the train". I wanted to be helpful, so I offered to give Jane a lift to the station in the morning. We had surprisingly been really kind to each other that morning. I was feeling this time out may just help us to get things on track. I drove to the station forecourt, leant over and kissed Jane goodbye, "I'll ring you later" she said, shutting the door and walking slowly toward the entrance of the station. I paused for a moment; she didn't look back and I drove off. In that moment something didn't seem right and as I drove off, I felt uneasy.

Later that day, I had a text, "I AM HERE, ALL OK".

I carried on with the day not having a great deal of time to think about Jane. I was missing her, but "this would do her good", I thought"

Two days later, Jane returned. She phoned and asked if I would meet her in the pub. I was happy she was back but why does she want to meet me in the pub? I grabbed my jacket and made my way down the stairs and took the short walk to the pub. Jane was sitting in the window, clearly looking uncomfortable. I ordered a drink and joined her. "You OK", I asked uneasily. "We need to talk", she said seriously. In that moment, my stomach twisted, I knew what was coming. "I am leaving you". My head was spinning, I could not understand what was happening. "I've done something stupid, and you won't want me anymore". I was confused, and tears were welling up in my eyes. "What have you done?" "I didn't go away on my own", Jane was shaking. My world was crashing, and I could not comprehend what Jane was telling me. "Who have you been away with?" I said angrily. Jane, just looked straight ahead, "Paul, I am sorry". I felt sick, I couldn't breathe. This cannot be happening. "I can't do this". I picked up my jacket and walked out into the cold evening. The tears were rolling down my face, my world was crashing at my feet, how could this be happening? I walked around the streets for what like felt hours. I took my phone out of my pocket and phoned the only person I thought could help. "Martin, it's Nigel, I need to see you", Martin could clearly hear my anguish. "Just come", I am here.

I walked the ten minutes to Martin's house, just hearing those words going through my head, "I am leaving you". By the time I reached Martin's house I was in even more of a state.

Martin was standing in his doorway, "hello dear boy, what is going on? Coffee?" Martin had a wonderful way about him, calm and composed. With coffee in hand, he invited me into his cosy study. I began trying to explain what had happened. My composure had gone, and, in between the words, I was just falling apart. Martin had travelled with Jane and I through all the turbulent times we had with Emma, and he had seen how we were falling apart. Martin listened, he then did what he did best, he prayed. We sat for a long time. "You don't want this to happen do you, you love Jane, and she loves you. God has brought you two together and he is with you in this". I began to pray through my tears, "God, be with me, help me in this mess". I had not prayed for days, I had been so busy with life, I had forgotten who I was, and who I was to God.

"I have to go home", I said. I knew that I had a fight on my hands, and I knew that God was with me.

I left Martin and started the walk home. I still felt sick, and my eyes were sore in the cold breeze. I stopped at the front door and paused. I felt a strange sense of strength come over me. I opened the door and walked in. Jane was sat in a chair by the window. "Where have you been?" she asked slowly. "I've been with Martin",

Jane didn't answer me, just looked out of the window. "I am sorry, I didn't want to hurt you". We sat in silence, for what felt like an eternity. As I looked at Jane, I could see how broken she was. The trauma of Emma going into care, the confrontations we had had between us, all the trial and trauma we had had were showing on her face. "I am so sorry too", what a mess this is.

We talked for hours, only pausing to go outside for cigarettes in between our lengthy discussions. "You can't leave", I said finally, "I love you". Jane looked straight into my eyes, "You don't want me now, and it's too late". "I know God brought us together, so yes, I do want you. I forgive you. I have been stupid, I didn't see how you were suffering".

Jane looked at me again, "You really do love me, don't you". I looked back at her, "of course I do".

In the early hours of the morning, Jane and I found each other again. The weeks and months that followed were a time of rebuilding, we had become closer than ever. We had both forgiven each other, not easily but faithfully. In that dark time, as we struggled through, we both knew that God was at work in us, we could feel his presence.

Martin was always on hand to keep us on track and of course, was continually praying. The strength we found would be needed as we continued to struggle with Emma in the many months that followed.

Chapter 5 - Street Pastors

Jane and I had already faced far too many challenges but we both felt that God was bringing opportunities through these hard times. We both felt a renewed strength and continued to look ahead.

The letterbox clicked and a thud announced the morning mail. Amongst the many bills, bills that always came for the many aspects of our business, a large see-through envelope lay on top “The Christianity”. Jane really enjoyed all the articles and looked forward to each edition.

This month’s offering had a picture of Les Isaac, the founder of a new Christian initiative, “Street Pastors”.

Jane immediately read the article and, in her excitement, announced, “We have to start this here”. She thrust the article under my nose and said, “Read this, its fab”. Within an hour, Jane was on the phone to various church leaders. “Have you heard of Street Pastors?” she continued to blurt out all the merits in some kind of hysterical excitement. Though always a polite response, most leaders were less than interested in this rather overexcited, crazy lady. Jane then decided to ask our own church leader. He was duly summoned to the café for a meeting. This was Jane’s meeting, so I decided to stay in the background. Jane explained what she was hoping for and looked at the leader for his response. “It’s a great idea, but the church is already over-committed to other things.” Jane was becoming frustrated at the lack of interest,

"Well, we will just have to do it ourselves". The leader was quite taken aback, and smiled, "Listen, I do think it's a good idea, we will support you through prayer, but please don't ask the church for any money".

I couldn't help laughing. I could hear the conversation and knew that Jane was not going to let this go. I tried to keep quiet and pretend I hadn't heard. Once the leader had left, Jane marched over to see me, "Well, if he doesn't want to know, I will find someone else who wants to help". I smiled and said, "Love, I know that this is good idea, and if God wants it to happen it will". I kissed her on the cheek and got back to filling the bar for the evening opening.

It was a day later the Jane's phone rang. "Hi, it's Peter here from St John's, I hear that you are interested in Street Pastors. I cannot help personally, but we have a new vicar in the town, who I believe has been involved with this".

Jane wasted no time in getting touch. Paul would certainly not be prepared for the call he received later that day. "Hello, my name is Jane, I want to start Street Pastors, and I have been told you can do it here". Her rather frantic and frenzied tones must have been rather overwhelming for a newly arrived vicar. Paul listened as Jane began to explain how she had walked the streets looking for her daughter, how she had prayed. Had there been Street Pastors, she may have had more support.

Paul agreed to meet with us and see if he would be able to help.

As always, we arranged a meeting in our café as Jane could always bribe people with food to get her own way. Paul duly arrived, and immediately we knew this was the guy who would help. A portly gent with a small goatee beard. Dressed casually and what felt like a laid-back approach. Paul sat and happily tucked into the freshly cooked bacon sandwich. "I arrived here a few weeks ago, I am the bishop's new Evangelist, and I was involved in Street Pastors in my last town". Jane smiled eagerly.

Paul continued, "I was only saying to my wife the other day, that it would be good to look at starting Street Pastors here. I really didn't think it would be so quick!"

When Jane got an idea, there was nothing stopping her. I think the dictionary definition of activist should be "Jane".

I looked at Jane, knowing that my turn was next. "You can do it too" she said excitedly.

The idea of me walking the freezing cold streets in the middle of the night was not appealing. I had already told Jane I would be quite reluctant to do it. Dealing with a load of drunks who would certainly not want some bible bashing Christian invading their Saturday night did not fill me with enthusiasm. "I'll make the tea back at base and be on the prayer team".

We continued to chat with Paul and started to hear how this ministry worked. The more I listened, the more I started to understand. A uniformed Christian presence on the streets, offering pastoral care to the night life of this town. It sounded crazy but at the same time, what an opportunity.

Many of the Christians we approached had the same view as I did at first, "you must be mad". Yet slowly we began to find support and a group was formed. It occurred to me that when I had said to God, "I want to serve you", God was answering that prayer. I became the joint coordinator of the group, helped to train the new volunteers, and began to look forward to our first night out. We were now very excited about this new venture.

The first night duly arrived and a TV crew, who had heard of this crazy idea joined us. Even the Bishop decided to join us for our first stint on the streets. Sporting our brand-new uniforms with a police radio, we had arrived. I had gone from reluctant volunteer to a short-lived celebrity. Jane hated the limelight and just wanted to get on with the job. So, I duly did the first interview, explaining what we were doing and the good we hoped to do. The interview ended, and, all smiles, I went back to my little group of volunteers. At that moment, a large police officer approached me." So, you want to do some good then", "Yes, of course" I said eagerly. "Well, just down the street there is a girl on her own, she has had too much to drink, I think you can go and sort her out". I headed off down the busy street and found the girl sitting on a bench. Her head between her knees, her long hair, covered in sick was covering her face. As I tried to get closer, I found myself slipping on the rest of what she had eaten on the floor. The pungent smell filled my nostrils, and the policeman, watching from a distance, was clearly enjoying the view. In that moment I had a moment of realisation, this is what service looks like, I felt humbled, the cameras and the media were unimportant. I had been humbled in a very powerful way. This is what ministry is about, being there for people at their worst moments. I helped to clean the young girl up and along with Jane, helped her to get home safely. Memories of my own filled my head, I knew what this was like, and I knew what these nights could do to people.

Street Pastors had arrived, and new chapter had begun.

Jane and I had been through a dark time of hurt and pain, we had learned a great deal about each other and were determined that our experience should be used for good. Over the months that followed we had so many conversations with people. Some were incredibly personal, people sharing with us their problems, their joy and even their deeply held secrets. To be able to share something of God's love with people was such a privilege. Already, our own life experiences were being used to help people through difficult times. All this, on a street, in the middle of the night. This was a powerful experience and one that led me to stop drinking completely. The days of alcohol, for me, were over.

Chapter 6 – From Business to Ministry

"Lehman collapse sends shock waves around the world"

The times headline on 16th September 2008 would not just have implications for financial institutions, it would have a massive impact on our little business.

The preceding months had shown signs that things were starting to go wrong. Business declined, and several corporate clients reduced their business. We were about to renew our contract with the arts centre, and a bombshell was about to explode.

I was putting on my apron, another day about to begin. 30 booked for lunch and an after-show supper to prepare for that night. It was going to be a busier day, after the slump of the last few weeks. I opened the letter, "Internal mail", the centre was owned by the council and any mail from them was delivered by their own couriers. It was our annual bill for the rent. I had to look twice and first thought it was an error. TOTAL DUE £23,000. "Jane, come and have a look at this", I needed a second pair of eyes. Jane was as horrified as much as I was, "that can't be right, ring them". I reached for the phone and got through to accounts. Yes Mr Perrott, "I am afraid that we have increased the rentals". I was becoming more distressed, "Why we were not told that our rent would go from £13,000 to £23,000, that's almost double". "We wrote to you over three months ago explaining that we were reviewing all our rents", the women's voice almost sounded infuriated that I would have the audacity to question it. My reply was equally as short, "yes, but you didn't say by how much and you certainly didn't say by this amount", I was now getting annoyed. "I am sorry Mr Perrott, if you are not happy you can write to complain". I was clearly not happy, but this rather unhelpful lady was not going to be of any help.

I put the phone down and turned to look at Jane. My face said it all, "Is this bad?" she said, looking worried. "I don't know, I'll have to write".

I did write, and I did get a response but not the kind I was hoping for. Our rent was almost doubling and if we didn't pay, we would have to close. Business was already slowing down, and we had lost another corporate client.

Jane and I knew that we would never be able to find the extra money needed and the cost of ingredients was also rising. We had wages to pay, tax to cover and this would only be the start. We agonised and prayed over the next few weeks and came to the decision that we would have to close. We had nothing else on the cards and if we left the café, we would not be able to afford the payments on our apartment either. We were in a particularly difficult situation. Yet, in this, Jane and I felt something good was going to happen.

We had only a few weeks to go, the café was closing, and we still didn't have anywhere to live and more importantly, no work.

Jane was in the yard at the back of the centre, lunch was over, and a crafty cigarette was on the cards. She popped outside and propped herself up against the wall. Anne, who worked next door in the betting shop, had joined Jane in the back yard for a smoke.

“Hi Anne”, Jane said, “How’s your day going?”, “Fine thanks, it’s busy, I’ve not had a break this morning”. Jane and Anne would often chat and pass the time before getting back to work.

“Jane, are you still looking for some work?” “Yes, it’s all getting a bit real now, and we’ve not found anything”. Anne, smiled, “well my friend runs a B&B down the road, and she’s looking for a manager”. “Can you give me her number; I’ll give her a call” Jane said hopefully.

Anne took a pen from her top pocket and wrote the number down, “Her name is Marie, just tell her I gave you her number”. Jane wasted no time in making the call and arranging a visit.

Jane decided not to tell me, just make the call and see what happens.

The B&B was not far from the arts centre, so Jane arranged to meet Marie later that day. Coming back into the café, Jane announced, “I’ve got a job”.

“Well, that was quick, you only went out for a smoke”, I laughed. Jane told me about the chat she had had with Marie on the phone, and I agreed to go along with her. The guest house was an old Victorian town house, over three floors with green ivy growing up the front. It was a pleasant looking building and being in the old town must have been quite busy. We were met by Marie, who opened the door with a big smile. "Welcome, come on in". She explained that her manager was leaving, and she needed someone very quickly. "The manager lives on site", so I can't afford not to have someone here". Jane and I looked at each other and smiled.

The job was clearly going to be hard work, changing beds, checking guests in and out, and generally keeping the house together. We were both familiar with hotels so this should be right up our street. It all sounded too good to be true. "I will pay you a small allowance each month and you can live here rent free". We were both excited and internally I was praising God for his provision. "Would you like to see the room you would have?" "Yes please", Jane was quite excited.

Marie walked ahead of us, down a narrow corridor to a door. "Lucy is in the process of moving out so it's a bit messy I'm afraid". As she opened the door, the smell hit me, the smell of an old ashtray. The room was almost in darkness as the curtains were closed. It was a large open plan room with a bay window at one end. I imagine it was knocked through at some point in the past to create one long room out of two. Half packed suitcases were strewn around the floor, and surprisingly a washing machine stood in the middle of the room. "Oh, that's Lucy's, don't worry she is taking that with her". As the curtains were pulled open, the light shone onto the dirty walls. My heart sank and I just looked at Jane. Marie continued to talk over what the job entailed, and we continued to look around the house. Thankfully all the guest rooms were well appointed and clean. This was clearly a nice guest house with rather unpleasant married quarters. We said our goodbyes and said we would be in touch. As Jane and I walked away, I looked at Jane. "There is no way on this earth that I am going to live in a room like that".

We lived in a brand-new apartment and there was no way I was going to swap luxury for that. "We may not have a choice, you know", Jane said softly.

Around a month later we moved in. Despite my initial misgivings, we made that room our home and would spend some very happy times there. It is amazing what some fresh paint and soft furnishings can do for a place. Rent free and as much bacon and eggs as we liked, on the house. We had accumulated several debts from the business, and this also gave us the opportunity to pay them off and get a clean slate. While Jane made beds, I worked in a local hotel and life was good. We continued with Street Pastors and our faith continued to grow. God was with us, and we were both happy. Emma was in foster care and though still causing Jane and me a great deal of worry, we were stronger as a couple and knew that God was walking with us.

This newfound freedom from the responsibility of being an employer, the endless worry of making ends meet soon brought us both a real sense of purpose. I still felt I needed more, something inside me kept nagging me and I couldn't shake it off. I looked forward to the weekends, a time when it felt I was really doing something for God. Being out on the streets at night, meeting people where they were at was something that made my heart skip. Not every shift brought an amazing experience, but ask any Street Pastor, and they will tell you, there was always one encounter that would make the night worthwhile.

It was one of those nights; we had always been told by the police not to use the "Q" word [quiet]. As we wondered the streets making our usual stops at the various clubs, the lack of folk around made the time go quite slowly. We were always received well by the door staff and customers alike. The initial misgiving of the community had disappeared. When they realised, we were there to help, not to preach, we were welcomed. We were often grabbed by enthusiastic club goers who wanted a selfie with the "pasta's".

It was around 2am, on a cold night. I had my thermals, thick socks and a scarf wrapped tightly around my neck, none of which kept the bitter wind from chilling my bones. We walked in teams of four, split into pairs. Jane was ahead of me with her partner. My radio bleeped, "hi we have a lady here and she needs some help", "Ok we are on our way".

As we entered the multi-storey, we could see Jane in conversation with a lady pushing a shopping trolley. The car park was a popular spot for rough sleepers, and normally at this time of night they were usually wrapped up in sleeping bags and duvets. As we approached, we realised that this was not our usual encounter.

This lady was clearly more elderly and certainly frailer than our average rough sleeper. Dressed in a long overcoat, woolly hat and wellington boots, she was an unexpected sight. The Tesco trolley she was holding onto clearly contained her life's belongings. Sitting on top of the carrier bags was a small dog, a scruffy looking terrier who was more than happy to receive some attention.

Jane was clearly filled with compassion for this lady and wanted to do what she could to help. This was an elderly lady, and she had no place in this dark and damp car park in the middle of the night. "How have you ended up here?" Jane asked quietly. "I have been kicked out and I just don't have anywhere else to go". "Can we try and help you?" "You can if you want, but don't hold your breath". She was clearly not expecting anything.

"Look, there's a hostel up the road, why don't you come with us, and we will see if they have some space". Reluctantly she agreed and we began the slow shuffle up the street. Jane chatting with her as they walked, it quickly became apparent that she had some mental health problems and a room for the night was not the only help she needed. After a short walk we arrived at the hostel. A large modern building that had once been a hotel. It was now owned by a large housing organisation. We knew we would have to wake someone, but this was urgent, someone of this age was vulnerable and should not be left alone.

Jane pushed the buzzer, there was no reply. Again, she pressed and after a short pause, there was a buzz and crackle from the intercom. "Yes, what do you want?" the voice was clearly annoyed as we must have interrupted their sleep.

"Hi, it's the Street Pastors, we have a vulnerable lady here and we could do with some help".

"Okay, give me a few minutes", they sounded annoyed, but Jane was determined that this lady needed help.

After what was a lot longer than hoped, a young man arrived. He looked through the glass without opening the door. "We don't have any beds, and we can't take her anyway". Jane was taken aback at his short and angry response. "Could she stay in your lounge until the morning?" "We can't take this woman, she doesn't keep to the rules, and we don't want her here".

Our new friend became annoyed, turning away clutching her trolley, she shouted at us, "I told you, and you are wasting your time".

There was clearly no point in arguing with the hostel worker and we turned to catch up with our new friend.

That night, all we could do was to buy a hot drink, a sandwich from a garage and make her as comfortable as possible in the car park.

The response from this hostel made me quite angry but Jane was almost in rage. “They didn’t even ask about the dog” she shouted angrily. “I could have understood refusing the dog, but her, I just can’t believe it”. Jane continued to get angry.

“Is there nowhere in this town for people like that?” Jane said when we arrived home later. “How many of our churches are locked up and empty every night?” I was quite stunned at Jane’s idea, “what are you thinking?” I asked. “We need a night shelter, somewhere that people like that can go”.

When Jane got an idea in her head, there was no stopping her, and by Monday morning she was on the phone again. After many calls she was put in touch with a local Anglican vicar who had been involved in homelessness issues. He worked as a chaplain in the town and Jane arranged to meet him the following day.

Jane wasted no time in telling him about the encounter at the weekend and the response from the hostel worker. “We need to get a night shelter, why can’t we use our churches?”

The vicar listened intently and smiled, “Jane, we have been trying to get something like this since the ’70s. I am sorry, but you will not get a night shelter here". Jane became more frustrated, "well I am sorry too, but people clearly haven't got enough faith for it". The vicar smiled again, "Jane, if you think you can do this, then try, but don't be too disappointed with the result".

Jane left his office with a new determination, there would be a night shelter, and she would make sure of it. Less than a year later, Jane had gathered other friends who really wanted to help, a local church opened its doors on a Friday night and soon welcomed their first rough sleepers. Other churches followed suit, and the night shelter was born.

The Street Pastors were going well, the night shelter was going from strength to strength, what else was there?

I still didn't feel that I was doing enough, there had to be more I could do, Jane and I knew that we had been called to serve, especially those who society had written off.

Chapter 7 – God Open the Door

Curled on the sofa in our lounge area of our little room, I was reading my Bible, I never really knew what to read. I had several books to help. "The Daily Bread" was my usual go-to book. Daily bible readings that generally had a little story to help me understand what I was reading. I had been to various bible studies through the church but, to be honest, I didn't really understand. Quite a lot of what I read was confusing and sometimes quite contradictory. If I were to really get to grip with this stuff, I needed more insight and then I would be able to do more. That is what I told myself. The idea came in that moment, Bible College, I need to go to Bible College. We were free to do it, I had no long-term commitments, and living in the B&B meant I could.

I began searching for various colleges, but it soon became more difficult than I had thought. I didn't like the idea of trying to study theology at some Christian University, I wasn't clever enough, and I was far too old. I just wanted to get a better knowledge of the Bible so that I could, in some way, see where God wanted me to be.

It took several weeks before I came across an advert for the Kings Bible College and Training centre in Oxford. A year to study the Bible and get involved in some mission. This was exactly what I wanted, it was close by, and I could go daily. The fees of just over

£2000 for year would be a struggle but I thought it was a possibility.

I talked it over with Jane and she agreed that it was a good idea, and I arranged to go for an open day.

The day arrived and we set off for Oxford just twenty or so miles from home. The college was housed within a large industrial estate on the outskirts of the city. This large building had been purchased by an independent church and half of the building was set aside for the college. On arrival we were greeted by one of the staff, "Welcome, are you both thinking of attending?" Jane was quick to reply, "Oh no, I leave that stuff to Nigel". The lady quickly replied while smiling, "Oh, we will have to see about that".

We spent a whole morning meeting staff and hearing talks about how this yearlong course worked. Alongside the academic studies, there was time to get involved in local missional projects. It sounded perfect and I knew this was going to be the right place for me. The staff were welcoming and, as the morning went on, it became more apparent to Jane that perhaps she was indeed meant to go. We left the college and drove home. All the time, the voice of that lovely lady echoed in Jane's ear "We will have to see about that, won't we".

Jane turned to me as we drove, "I think I should go". Rather than happy with her suggestion I felt a little annoyed, "This was my idea, something for me". Jane could see I was a little upset. “We can’t really afford for me to go, let alone both of us”

I had hoped that Jane would continue to work, and I would commute to the college. This wouldn’t work if we were both to go. Deep down inside, I knew that this would not work. If Jane wanted to go too, we would need a different plan, we didn’t have one. Disappointed, I let the idea go and, as the weeks went by, I put any idea of college to one side.

This newfound faith was now starting to mature and life continued to offer some unexpected situations.

On one such occasion it was a phone call from South Africa. A man called Wayne; he had found our telephone number from the internet while looking for accommodation for a six-month work trip. “Hi, I am coming to England and need somewhere to stay”. Jane in her normal enthusiastic way replied, “Oh, I think me and Jesus can help you do that”.

The reply from Wayne was quite unexpected.

I am a Christian, and I felt God tell me that I should ring you” Jane shouted down the phone, “Praise the Lord”, we can help”.

This completely random phone call led him to us in the spring, he took a room in the B&B and a new friendship began. Having spoken on the phone to this larger-than-life character, I was expecting a large well-built and loud Christian to arrive on our doorstep.

The doorbell rang, and Jane rushed to the door to greet him. In front of us was a slender built man, shorter than me with head of jet-black hair. Wayne was of Indian descent, and we both took an instant liking to him. He worked for a large pharmaceutical company and had been sent to England to help with a new product.

We set about helping him to find his feet and arranging transport to his work. It was clear that he would need a car as his work was a forty-minute drive away.

At the time I had an old car which needed some attention as it had an electrical fault. "If you can fix it, you are welcome to it". Wayne laughed and said, "Oh don't worry, if God wants me to have it, it will be fine".

I took Wayne outside and showed him the car, a Ford Escort with rather rusty wheel arches and a faded vinyl roof. Wayne looked at the car, "This is fine, thank you so much" he sat in the seat, and I passed him the key. "Thank you, Lord, for your provision" he prayed, he popped the key in the slot and turned, the engine started first time. "It does sometimes start", I said, not really thinking one little prayer would fix this problematic little car. It did occasionally start first time but when I needed to get anywhere it would die on me. Wayne used that car for six months without a single problem. It always started first time and never had a breakdown. When the day came for him to leave, he gave me the car back. I sat in the car, turned the key and a flashing light appeared on the dashboard "ENGINE MANAGEMENT". Wayne laughed and I just shrugged my shoulders in disgust. We had forged a great friendship with Wayne and kept in touch.

He eventually invited us to come and stay with his family and even suggested that we could attend a college in South Africa while staying with him. The prospect of moving to Cape Town and attending college sounded amazing. I looked at various options and it certainly seemed to be a possibility. We prayed and said to God, "If this is something you want us to do, please open the door, if not, please close it".

It was around this time we were finding church life a little difficult. We were still feeling uncomfortable in church, we never really felt we fitted in. We changed church twice in a year, hoping that this time, we would find the right place to call home. Eventually we found ourselves in a small church which had not long arrived in the town. We met in a school hall, not dissimilar to the one we had first joined. We knew some of the congregation through Street Pastors and felt at home and welcome. One evening we were with a couple from the church. As we chatted, they told us that they had attended a Bible college. I told them about our disappointment of not being able to go. To my amazement, Tony piped up "KBCTC" that is the college we attended". Tony explained that the college was owned by the church we were now attending. Salt and Light Ministries had several churches around the country and our church was one of the new ones just being planted.

A few weeks later we had been invited to a "Pampered Chef' evening for a church night out. It was basically a fun social evening making breads and other pastries using equipment that was sold as part of the Pampered Chef range. It was great fun, and we enjoyed getting to know the rest of the church. At the end of the evening, the Pastor approached us and asked to speak to us in private. Had we done something wrong, were we going to be thrown out for being too odd for this church?

We waited for people to leave and sat down with the Pastor. "I have been talking about you this week", Jane and I looked at each other waiting for the bad news. "My wife sits on the governor's board at our college", Jane and I looked at each other again, now looking even more puzzled. "I hear you were interested in attending the college". "Yes" I said, "it was just an idea, and we really can't afford it". The Pastor beamed, "Well this week, the college has received an anonymous donation for a student to attend the college". They have asked that it goes to someone in one of the new churches". I was in shock, excited and ready to say yes straight away. Then I had to remind myself that Jane wanted to go as well. I had realised at this point, that Jane really should go with me and a wave of disappointment came over me again. "Can we have a think about this please?" Our Pastor agreed and we arranged to meet in a few days to talk some more.

As Jane and I drove home, we both felt an excitement and began to work out what we should do.

“If we both go, we will have to give up the B&B”, how can we afford to live?” I just couldn’t see how we could make it work.

Jane as always was the voice of reason, “Well if God wants us to go, we will find a way”. I had now learned that Jane had far more faith than I did, and I was not going to challenge it.

Later that week we arrived at the Pastor’s house, our minds made up that we would politely decline their offer and thank them for thinking of us. We were invited in and took our seats in a comfy leather sofa. “So, what do you think?” he asked. “We would love to go, but a donation for me is not enough, Jane really wants to go, and we just can’t afford it, even with the donation”. The Pastor smiled and turned to look at his wife. She too smiled and said, “We knew you were going to say that we have prayed about this, and we agree you should both go”. I was shaking with excitement and held Jane’s hand tightly. “The church will pay the rest of the fees, and you can live in one of the college houses”.

Jane’s words were in my head, “If God wants us to go…”

So that was it, we were off to Bible college. We knew that we would still need to find a small income to buy food and generally live, but if God had done this, we knew that we could do it.

God had firmly shut the door on Cape Town, and we were off to Oxford. Not quite the blue skies and sun we were thinking of, but a new chapter, nonetheless.

We remain great friends with Wayne and hope that one day soon we will finally get to Cape Town!

Chapter 8 – College Life and a Trip Abroad

At age 43, I was the one of the oldest in our cohort, the youngest being just 18. I certainly felt more like a dad than I did a student and soon realised that I knew a lot less than I thought. The lectures quickly became very theory-led and some of the discussions that followed were equally alien to me. I have never really been a person who could concentrate; my school reports would often say I was a child who did not listen. I would often drift off in my own thoughts and though my face looked as though I were engaged, I was somewhere else. Jane too, was not the academic, but loved the times of prayer and worship. She would soon find her feet getting involved in various community activities.

My first few weeks at college started to feel more like school and I found myself drifting in the same way I did all those years ago.

It was one such day that I would realise I would need to wake myself up. New Testament lecture on the teaching of Jesus.

The voice of the lecturer was echoing in my head, I had no idea what was being said as my mind was clearly not engaged. I was more interested in looking out of the window and daydreaming. The lecturer looked straight at me, clearly thinking that my glazed expression was listening to what was being said. "What do think Nigel"? To my dismay, I was being asked a question about something I had no idea about.

I stuttered, not wanting to seem like a complete idiot, "The Devil", I responded. The look from the lecturer was clearly puzzled, and the other students, too, had no idea what I was talking about. "Interesting" the lecturer replied, "How do you see the devil in the feeding of the five thousand?" I must confess, I can look engaged when I am not and I can also blag my way out of difficult situations too, "Well the devil clearly wanted everyone to go hungry". I was quite impressed that I was able to respond, even though it was completely ridiculous. The lecturer politely moved on and, though he must have thought I had lost the plot, didn't challenge me on the response. I felt I had got away with my lack of concentration and told myself to try and engage better in the future.

Days and weeks passed by, and my concentration did improve, and I started to get a better understanding of what was going on. Even at this early-stage I just wanted to learn enough that would help me to be a better witness to people who knew nothing of Jesus. I always found the practical work far easier and the opportunity to do some mission work in the community so much more rewarding. Part of this took place on a deprived estate on the outskirts of the city. Seeing people whose lives were shattered due to poverty and addiction tugged at my heartstrings and I knew that this was where God wanted me to be. So, when the day came to learn about a mission trip abroad, I was less than happy.

The college had links to a Christian outreach in North Africa. A Muslim country that does not look favourably on Christians who declare Jesus as their saviour.

Jane was quite happy to go, but I was not. “There is no way I want to do this, my calling is here, in the UK”. I decided to speak to my Pastor and explain that this was not a good Idea. That evening, I phoned him to let him know I would not be going. I had all my excuses ready and made the call. The response I received was not what I hoped for. “So, God has called you to work in the UK?” “Yes” I replied, “I know that there are so many people living with problems here, and this where God wants me”. My Pastor listened and with the odd, “yes and no”, seemed to understand. “Yes, you are making some good points, but have you tested that call?” I was slightly taken aback. “Nigel, sometimes you need to understand other people’s worldview in order to see your own”. I was feeling uncomfortable as I was clearly not getting my own way. “But”, as I began to speak, he cut me off, “Nigel, you are going”. I could feel his smile down the phone. I quickly realised that my objections were being dismissed, and my arguments were not going to change his mind.

A few weeks later I found myself at the airport waiting to board the plane, and some hours later was carrying a backpack in 40 degrees heat. We journeyed to a small village in the mountains. After a few hours of tarmac road, we found ourselves on a dusty street, bumping our way up a steep hill, passing orange and yellow concrete buildings. Eager children ran alongside our minibus, shouting greetings that I didn't understand but their smiles made us feel welcome.

Our accommodation was basic but comfortable, several dormitories surrounding a large open dining area. This would be our home for the next few weeks. The village was clearly poor, and several dilapidated houses lined the narrow street where we stayed. The centre itself catered for British tourists who came to walk and climb in the area. "Team building" has never been something I have enjoyed, yet this trip was designed to do exactly that. I still held a few grudges about my newfound Christian family. I had started to learn what grace was about and this was something I needed in much quantity. I was still recovering from our last adventure in Wales - a camping trip aimed at helping us solve problems. The leader of my group announcing that we needed to find a dry bit of field to set up our tents. On a normal day that may have seemed a sensible suggestion. It was, however, January, it was pouring with rain, and we were in the Brecon Beacons. God clearly has a sense of humour when he teaches us about grace.

I was now on another continent, in soaring heat with the same group of people. The idea that I was somehow to gain some theological insights was far from my mind. Jane on the other hand relished the whole idea and could not wait to join in.

Our first adventure began at sunrise the next day. Our guide gathered us in the dining area for a briefing. “We are going on a trek and a short climb”. As people eagerly listened to his instructions, my inner self began to cry out. A whole three days of walking and nearly killing myself scrabbling through the countryside in soaring heat, “Oh joy”.

Kit was gathered and we set off up the hill leaving the centre behind us. As we reached the top, we could see the sun rising over the village below. A strange sense of purpose came over me and I stretched out my hand to Jane and we began the long trek toward the mountains. The heat of the day made the walk exhausting and after eight hours we finally arrived at the base camp. We set about erecting tents and preparing meals. Jane has always been an organiser, and she found herself on cooking duty. As we tucked into our meals Matt, the leader, began to explain how the next day would pan out. We would be set into two teams. The first would climb and the other stay behind and get meals ready for our return. I had no intention of spending a whole day climbing and suggested that Jane do the climb. “I went down a cave in Wales, you can do this”, she looked at me with a reassuring smile. “It’s not really climbing, just a hard walk”, Jane smiled even more. Something inside me told me that I should give it a go.

Reluctantly I agreed and joined the climbing group.

The following morning, as the sun began to rise, I kissed Jane and set off with the rest of the group. I was the oldest person in the group and my legs and back told me so. Jane was right, no ropes, just lots of very hard walking, the air was getting thinner, and I began to struggle. The hours passed and the summit seemed so far off. Finally, after a few hours, we reached what I thought was the summit. We had all collapsed, taking a much-needed break.

Matt gathered us together and began to explain what was next. "Just a few hundred feet and we will be there"

My heart sank, I can't do any more, I was breathless, and every bone in my body was aching. "The first person to reach the summit has to read this passage from Isaiah". Matt was holding a small Bible in his hand. "Isaiah 52:7-9".

My face must have said it all and Matt came over to me. "Listen, you have done so well, you can be proud of what you have achieved. You can wait here while the others finish". This guy was kind, he could see my pain and yet I could not allow this. There was no way I was going to come this far and just sit here and watch these guys race ahead. I stood up, a new sense of strength came over me. I looked up, it was steep, and the loose rocks slipped under my feet. I started walking, pushing on through the pain in my legs. Leaning forward I just kept on going, then as the last of the rocks slipped under my feet, I was there. I collapsed looking down at the faces of those below. I had done it, not only that, but I had also been the first. The sense of achievement was overwhelming, Matt handed me the bible and I began to read.

"*How beautiful on the mountains are the feet of those who bring good news*"

Matt came over and sat with me. "We hear so often that we must climb mountains in life, for many people, they never physically do it, today you have learned that lesson and learned it well. Through God all things are possible".

I was humbled yet again and felt such a peace come over me. As others came over to congratulate me, I was not proud but humbled that God indeed was with me.

On the long walk back to camp I felt I had learned a lesson that would be taken home. The remaining time on our trip was spent helping the local school and generally helping around the village. On our last day we were given the opportunity to take some time out. On the edge of the village there was a small olive grove. We took our Bibles and spent time praying and reading. It occurred to me that the scenery would have not been dissimilar to that of the days of Jesus. As I sat leaning against a tree, I noticed streams of people walking up the track from the village. It had been market day, and they were all heading home. Lines of donkeys carrying the things that had been bought and sold during the day.

Stood at the side of the track was Matt. He had lived in the village for 25 years and clearly knew many of the people. One of our group had brought their baby along on the trip and Matt was holding the small child as the people passed. Some of the women had seen him and came over to see this little bundle of joy. They were all smiles and clearly enjoyed making a fuss. As I watched, Matt was talking, I had no idea what was being said, he was fluent in the language and was very much at home. As I continued to watch, I could see how much love he had for those people, a love that was strong. He had spent a lifetime with these people, getting to know them, befriending them and loving them. His face said it all, God had broken his heart for these people.

This trip, the one I never wanted to do, had taught me some valuable lessons about God's love and his purposes for our lives. I had to travel to North Africa to learn them, and now learned, they would be such a big part of what was to follow when we returned to England.

Chapter 9 – South to North

Jane and I both managed to get through the academic work, passing each module, which often came as a shock. We were both more focused on the practical and had been given the nickname of "The Pioneer Perrott's". I really appreciated the insights to the Bible, understanding more about God through the scriptures would prove to be invaluable. Alongside this, getting out into the community was always such a blessing, being around those on the edge of community just seemed so refreshing. Jane had a real heart for those living with difficulties and just shone when she met people. She spent time in a local community centre and within a few months was 'mothering' many of those who came through the door. We both knew that this was something we needed to do when we returned home after college.

Our last term brought us what was going to be the most powerful experience of our lives and things were never going to be the same.

Our course had flown by, and the weeks and months just seemed to be a blur. One morning we had gathered in our lecture room and our tutor began to explain how our last month would run. We had already spent time serving in some areas around Oxford, particularly one estate where high crime rate, drug addiction and family breakdown were all common place. There was no formal church, and the main work was done by a couple who lived on the estate. It was so refreshing to see how their presence was making a difference in the area. We both knew that this was something we felt being called to and, when the course was over, we had planned to return home and look for a similar place to start some outreach.

We were now being given the opportunity to choose a topic we could explore in more detail over the month. We both felt that "Church Planting & Evangelism" would help us discern what we should do after college. This would involve spending time in the north of England where several different styles of mission were happening. Our trip would involve working with a group from "The Eden Project".

The project is overseen by the Message Trust and focuses on community engagement. The leader of the group we would work with lived on an estate and worked from a local church. Neither of us had any idea what was involved, but it was something we felt we needed to investigate further.

During the time at college my little car had died, and we had been gifted an old estate car to get around. It was great, and the fact I had to use an old broom handle to keep the boot open just added to its charm. The old diesel engine always started with a black cloud of smoke but always went where we wanted it to go without problem. The five-hour car journey from Oxford would take it to its limit, but it didn't let us down.

It was a warm sunny afternoon when we finally arrived. We had been invited to stay in a church member's home. They were away on holiday and had left a key with our host from the local church. We were slightly taken aback as we pulled into the drive of this handsome three-storey Victorian house - nothing like we were expecting, and the inside was equally beautiful. This was going to be in stark contrast to where we would find ourselves the next day.

There were four of us on the trip and we crammed ourselves into our car and followed the directions we had been given to get to the estate. The rather grand houses were behind us and we found ourselves on a council estate only ten minutes' drive away.

When built around fifty years ago, the estate would have been a joy to move to, in contrast to the terraced houses built in the town centre a century earlier. Fifty years on, this estate was showing its age. Lack of investment and the decline in industry had thrown the area into poverty. The Eden project had recently started in the area, and we would be working alongside the team. Over the course of a week, we helped tidy gardens, attended drop-in coffee mornings, and generally had time to experience what life was like in the area.

It was a meeting with another church member that would start to spark our thoughts. We had been invited for an evening meal at their home.

Sarah and Chris were newlyweds and lived in a little house near the town centre. Sarah's father was the Pastor of the church. This young couple had a passion for their town and were determined that God's love be known, especially those who lived on the margins. Chris was clearly well educated and worked in accounts, while Sarah was a primary school teacher. We were ushered into the small dining room, "We thought you might be hungry after your day". We all were, and very tired. Early mornings and late nights were becoming the norm on this trip. "We've ordered a "Parmo", you need to try this" We had heard people talk about the "Parmesan" but had no idea what it was. A few minutes later, the bell rang, and a delivery driver handed over four pizza boxes. The boxes were placed on the table, "Ok dig in" on inspection, the 12" box was filled with a flat piece of chicken breast, covered in melted cheese. The chicken breast is flattened, covered in breadcrumbs, deep fried, then covered in a white sauce and grated cheese. It is finished under a grill. It was huge and we struggled to get through it all. Not an ounce of Parmesan cheese, so we had no idea where it got its name. It is a local dish and certainly isn't the healthiest of meals!

As we made small talk about our day, Chris began to describe their vision and ambitions for ministry in the town. "The Eden group are doing really well, and the work is great, we want to see them do something similar on one of the poor estates near to us".

Jane and I glanced across the table at each other, I think our look was seen by Chris who laughed. “Oh, don’t think you have seen anything yet, The Banks is far worse”.

I think we were all quite shocked that there could be anything worse than we had seen so far.

After we had eaten, Chris took us over to the “Banks”. Driving quickly around the estate, we soon realised that this was indeed, far worse. What we saw that evening would open both eyes to a need that would change the course of both our lives.

Chapter 10 - Testing the Call

What we had seen over this short visit had opened our eyes, a place of abject poverty and yet a place where the people understood each other. There was a sense of "all in this together". On our journey back to Oxford, we were both quietly contemplating what this meant to us. The friends we travelled with were only too keen to return to the safety and comfort of college. They were in their late teens and from quite privileged backgrounds and seeing some of the issues was quite harrowing for them. I think they were more than happy to leave.

By the time Jane and I returned to our shared house in Oxford we were suddenly in full blown confusion mode. What did this mean? Why was the tug on our hearts so strong?

By this time, we had only a few weeks left before our course ended and we knew that we needed to explore this call further. The weeks rolled by and our graduation came and went. In this time, we continued to pray and felt we needed to take another visit to the North. Our first visit had been well planned: who we would visit, what we would do, and the people we would meet. We decided that if we were to see the place without guides, without the organised agenda, we may see if this call was real or just enthusiastic musings.

We made a few calls and arranged to stay at the same house that we had stayed on our last visit. The five-hour drive back up the M1 dragged, and Jane and I felt a sense of excitement but at the same time some trepidation. "We must be mad", Jane said, while watching the endless motorway signs flash past.

By the time we arrived it was getting dark. Parking on the drive after the long trip, we sat in the car and prayed. "Lord, if this is you, show us"

We climbed the steps to the house, unloaded our bags and put the kettle on. Sitting in the kitchen, my eyes sore from the long drive, Jane announced, "let's go now", "I'm tired, it's dark, and what do you think you are going to see? "I don't know, I just think we may a get a feel of what it's like at night".

Reluctantly, I grabbed my coat, and we walked out to the car, "Can you remember the way?" Jane asked, "Nope", I said smiling. This was true, we had been taken by car to the estate on our last visit and I genuinely couldn't remember which way to go. It was now dark as I pulled out of the drive and started my way up the main road. "This doesn't look right" I said, becoming more irritated. We spent half an hour driving around and getting lost until I just gave up. We drove back to the house feeling deflated. We wanted this trip to be incognito, we couldn't phone anyone, and the lack of satnav didn't help. We both suddenly felt a wave of disappointment; had we come all this way for nothing? The air of enthusiasm we had on our previous visit was gone.

The next morning, we were up early, the much-needed sleep had given us both some fresh energy. "Ok, I turned left out of the drive last night, I'm turning right today, and if we don't find our way in half an hour, we should just leave". Jane smiled at my suggestion, and we set off to a brand-new chapter.

As the road came to a sharp bend I saw a turning on the right, something inside me told me to take it, as the car turned, we found ourselves on a long straight road, and I followed until we reached a crossroads. I stopped at the lights, and there in front of us was Banks Road. It had taken less than 5 minutes to arrive.

We parked the car and looked at each other and together we said "OK, let's do this". Inside, I had no idea what that meant, Jane the ever faithful and more enthusiastic climbed out of the car. Banks Road is long, terraced houses line the wide expanse, some neatly kept gardens and others filled with car parts and broken plastic toys. We walked slowly down the road; it was still early, and the road was quiet. As we made our way, we realised that half the estate had been demolished, some houses remained, and the dark green screens covering all the windows gave an insight to their impending doom. Large piles of bricks lay scattered across what was once a bustling street.

As we continued our journey, two men appeared in front of us, walking quickly with air of urgency in their steps. Two or three paces behind was a small child, following as quickly as her little legs would allow. Just as they came closer to us, they veered off, made their way up a path, knocked once on a door and entered. The door slammed shut, leaving the little girl outside, she sat down on what looked like an old beer crate. We carried on walking, walking slowly, and praying under our breath. As we glanced over to the pile of bricks, we saw more children playing. The scene reminded me of those old post-war photos of bombed out London streets.

What did these kids have to do, where was the hope?

In this moment, my mind went back to North Africa, Matt, standing in the olive grove, his heart broken for the people. Jane and I looked at each other, "Yes", we said. Another hour passed as we journeyed through the estate, the odd "hello" and the occasional, strange look at this odd couple wandering the street.

It had taken just a couple of hours to know that God was indeed calling us here, and that would be the easiest thing to explain. Well, that's what we thought and yet what followed would be some of the most upsetting times of our newfound faith.

The following morning, we went to church, the one that had hosted us on our first visit. We met the Pastor and explained why we had returned. The meeting went well, and he and his wife seemed thrilled that we felt called to the estate. The church was some distance from the Banks and, though the estate was well known, it had no presence there.

We said our farewells and travelled the long road back south. It was now going to get tough; we were ill-prepared for what was going to follow.

Back in the south we were filled with a new sense of purpose and enthusiasm when we returned to our church. We were received well and one of the church members had given us a room in their house as we had now left Oxford.

We arranged to meet our Pastor and his wife so that we could properly explain what had happened. We had already written several letters, keeping them in the loop of what we were experiencing. We were both excited to share what God had put on our hearts and to thank them for their kindness in arranging the opportunity to go to college.

It was a warm sunny afternoon when we arrived at their house, and we were ushered into their lovely garden with a large table in the centre where we were offered some cold juice.

Though we had been here many times before, something felt wrong, the normal smiles were replaced with rather formal pleasantries.

The pleasant conversation didn't last long. "I'm going to say this quietly, as I don't want our neighbours to hear what I am saying", the Pastor's wife's face looked flushed and angry. "You are both being quite ridiculous, God is not calling you anywhere". I could see that Jane already had tears in her eyes. "You are betraying our goodwill and have let us down badly". I wanted to blurt out my defence, but my mind just couldn't make sense of what was being said. "We sent you to college so that you would return here and serve this church, you have let us down and badly".

The Pastor then looked me in the eye with the same disdain. "So, you are going to go up North to help the poor, you have no support". I tried to get the right words out, but the words just kept coming. "So, are you going to be the solution to all those problems or just part of the problem?"

As he paused, I felt a sense of peace, "No" I said with some determination, "we will be both".

We left their house feeling completely drained and disheartened, the feeling of doubt and rejection had really affected both of us. As we sat in the car, Jane burst into tears.

I put the key in the ignition, paused, "Jane, I love you, and I know we are doing the right thing". Jane looked at me, "yes, I know".

A side note:
It would be years later when we met the Pastor and his wife again, forgiveness was shared, wounds were healed, and a relationship was restored.

Chapter 11 - Up North

The fanfare of leaving never arrived, bar a few close friends, and Martin of course, to say goodbye, we set off North. The one thing the Pastor had been right about was the fact we didn't have any support. The church we were leaving didn't support us and the one we were going to were not fully committed either.

We had left the security of work, we had nowhere to live, and our funds had dried up during a year at college in Oxford. On the day we left, we had a full tank of diesel and a bank account with the total sum of £75. I smiled and said to Jane, this is like something out of that Blues Brothers film.

"It's a hundred and six miles to Chicago, we've got a full tank of gas, half a pack of cigarettes, its dark, and we're wearing sunglasses"

Jane laughed, and in that moment, we had some humour, we would need a lot of it. It was over 250 miles to travel, we had both given up cigarettes, and it was raining.

Yet, in the humour, there was a seriousness that we couldn't ignore. God had provided for us over the last year, the odd envelope with notes from anonymous donors left through the letterbox, kind parents, and friends who wanted to help. This was different, we were embarking on what would be a huge step of faith.

Another five-hour drive up the long road north and we arrived in the town. The Pastor of the church had spoken with a friend, and they agreed to let us use their caravan for a few days. We met them in their little terrace house in the centre of the town and they took us to the site where it was parked. After a short drive we found ourselves in the heart of the countryside. A stone's throw from the town and yet so far from what we had come for. The site was used to store caravans when not in use, so the amenities were few and far between. It was a roof and that was all that mattered. Our priority had to be money, without it, we would indeed have become part of a problem and be of no help at all. Our first break came from the local paper. CLEANERS REQUIRED. A local cinema was looking for early morning cleaners and Jane duly applied. A 5.30am start, vacuuming popcorn and general cleaning around the complex. Though only part time, it was a start. It was autumn and a caravan in Yorkshire was not going to be a long-term solution. An opportunistic conversation from a church member led us to house sit while they were on holiday. It was back in the town and not far from the cinema. A two-week break with flushing loos and a comfy bed was much appreciated.

We continued to write prayer letters and updates to some of our friends. Most of them thought we were mad but knew us well enough that they were behind us.

The letterbox clacked one morning and as I picked up the mail, I saw my name on the front of a large brown envelope. Who could be sending me this here? I opened the envelope and found a CD case and as I fumbled to open it, I realised it was full of cash. "You need somewhere to live, I hope this helps" Tim.

Jane had a month's wage, and the £300 stuffed into an old CD case meant we could start to look for somewhere to rent. As we trolled through the local paper looking for the right place, I came across an advert for a job. SANDWICH DELIVERY DRIVER. I rang the number and arranged to meet the owner. The premises were located on a local industrial estate, and I drove over the same day. In amongst the many small industrial units there was a small catering outlet. A few jiffy vans parked outside, a man holding a large hose was washing down the floor of the unit. It was 4'oclock in the afternoon and the busyness of the day had passed.

After a brief chat, no interview, just a few short questions about driving I was asked to come at 7am the next day. I immediately liked the no nonsense approach of this guy, down to earth and straight to the point. "You got a licence?", "yes", "is it a full one?", "yes of course!" "Do you know anything about catering?" "Yes, I used to run a café". "Great, you'll do, I'll see you in the morning".

The following morning, I drove into the industrial estate and parked up. A young girl came bounding out to greet me, I'm Sharon, and you're with me. I followed her around like a lost sheep as she barked orders at the catering staff, "six parmos and four corned beef pies for ten o'clock".

"Get in" she laughed.

Over the next few minutes, she described what she did and tried to explain the route, who wanted what, and many other things I can't remember. Her quick-fire voice was enthusiastic and very confusing. We travelled around the docks, car dealerships and other industrial buildings, the horn would sound, and she would jump out to a queue of hungry workers. The first couple of hours flew by, as did the many streets and buildings. My head was popping with the speed at which the words came out of Sharon's mouth and at the same time I was trying to remember this route. We headed back to the base and collected the various hot lunches needed for the second run. As we left the building, Sharon laughed and said, "Will you remember all this?" I laughed and said, "Yeah, it will be fine". "Liar she shouted", still laughing. "Don't worry, I've written it down and you will be with me for a couple of days"

Sharon turned out to be such a lovely person and I was free to tell her what Jane, and I wanted to do, we talked about Jesus and to my joy she soaked it up without a word of criticism. "That's what a church should be doing" she said, while taking another corner at a speed that made me close my eyes.

With both Jane and I working within weeks of arriving we were able to get enough money to rent a house. It turned out to be far more difficult to rent on our chosen estate, the houses just didn't come up for rent and those who lived there had no intention of moving. Half the estate had already been demolished, and it was looking increasingly difficult to move there. We both knew that we couldn't help if we didn't live there, we had to find a home there. In the meantime, we found a local landlord who rented us a terrace house in the streets. Think Coronation Street, and you won't be too far off. Two rooms downstairs and a small bathroom off the kitchen. The tiny and narrow staircase led to two small bedrooms. It was cosy, clean and comfy. Finally, we had a base from which we could set our sights on the Banks.

Between us, we both earned enough to get by, the odd one-off job here and there certainly helped to keep us fed and watered. We would often drive up to the estate and pray; it felt right, and we knew that eventually, when the time was right, we would move there.

Chapter 12 - The House on the Banks

The months passed and we became friends with people from the local church we had visited and had now started to attend. The Pastor and his wife were very supportive of what we were doing, but their involvement was limited. We felt at home in this church, and we met other like-minded folk who wanted to see the work on the Banks start.

One afternoon, we decided to take another prayer walk around the estate. We parked up and began walking up Banks Road. As we reached the top of the road, two young women were sat on the kerb in deep conversation. Jane always made the first move, "Hi, how are you?"

"Um, ok". Both girls looked a little worse for wear but were quite happy to chat.

A conversation was struck up and we mentioned we were looking for a house to rent. "You could buy that one if you want", we turned to look, and behind us was a large house with an open drive. An AUCTION billboard was nailed to the fence. "I think it's up for £40,000", the girl said. "I live next door". Jane the ever faithful smiled and said, "If God wants me to have it, we will" I laughed, "Love we don't have 40p at the moment, I don't think we can stretch to £40k". Undeterred, Jane continued. What do you like to drink? Puzzled the girl said, "Lambrini". "Ok, well, when we move in, I'll bring you a bottle".

We left the two girls on the kerb, slightly bemused at this strange couple who wanted to move to the area.

The next day, Jane rang the estate agents, much to my disapproval, "I've told you; we can't get a mortgage, it just isn't going to work".

Jane had her sights set and nothing was going to put her off. Putting the phone down, she looked at me, "All sorted, we are going to view it tomorrow". There was no point in telling Jane it wasn't going to work and the next day we drove back for the viewing.

"Do you know what, I'm going to stay in the car", I looked at Jane and she smiled as she left the car. Ten minutes later she was back. "It's a bit of a mess, but it's massive and will do us". The house had been unoccupied since the owner moved to a care home, and it was decided to put it up for sale.

"Love we don't have the money", Jane just smiled, I'm going to ring the estate agents and tell them that if it doesn't sell, we will rent it".

Again, I just stayed silent and allowed Jane the space to do what she thought was right. The idea she had, did sound feasible. Jane phoned the agents and duly passed on the message. The following week, the day of the sale, the agent rang Jane. "The house has not gone to auction and has been taken off the market, due to unforeseen circumstances", they couldn't say any more.

That evening, Jane was at a prayer evening at the church and one of those attending spoke to Jane. "You wanted to rent that house on the banks, didn't you?" "Yes, but it's not for sale or rent now",

"Well, the old man who owned the house has just died", Jane sprang up and, without thinking, shouted "Praise the Lord!" "Oh sorry, I didn't mean it to come out like that". "Don't worry the girl said, I know the family and he was very old. I know his son in law, John, and he knows you are interested in renting. She handed Jane a note with his telephone number.

By the time Jane came home she was almost off the planet with excitement. As she explained, my heart skipped but at the same time felt a little shame at my lack of faith. The following day, we rang John and arranged to meet him at the house.

John was a big man, an engineer by trade, something to do with steel, and was standing in the porch waiting for us when we arrived.

Jane hadn't been wrong; the house was in a bad way. Stepping through a glass porch area we entered the hallway, thick Axminster carpet fitted wall to wall. The walls carefully covered in embossed bright green wallpaper with matching green skirting boards. Stairs ahead led to three bedrooms and a bathroom. Walking up we were greeted by a small landing and a large bathroom. Bright green tiles from floor to ceiling complimented with a matching bath, sink and loo, all in the customary bright green. Each bedroom with its own fitted wardrobe and thick heavy carpet. The bedrooms at least were painted with what was once magnolia, now looking rather more off grey. Returning down the stairs we entered the kitchen, dark green Lino, with matching dark green worktops and units. The Belling fitted stove was, of course, green with shiny brass handles and knobs. The kitchen itself was an extension on the back of the house and was big enough for a seating area and large dining table. In the lounge, the room was framed with a large bay window, also carefully crafted green wallpaper adorned the walls.

“The old man was a decorator in his day”, John explained with a huge grin across his face. He continued as he laughed, “It’s over the top but in its day, it was all quality stuff, and he spent a small fortune on the place”. John was right, though the colours were over the top, everything was professionally done. I’m sure in the early ’80s this would have looked great, but not so today.

“If you want to paint over the green, that’s fine”, Jane piped up straight away, “Yeah, I think we will”. “I’ll sort some paint for you, not a problem. “I know the place is a bit of mess and needs a good clean, but if you clean and paint the place I won’t worry about a bond, and we can sort rent out later”.

The place was a little smelly, dust and mothballs, yet this house was perfect, and we knew that this was a gift.

That evening we went to the supermarket and picked up a bottle of Lambrini and went to meet our new neighbour. “Jane walked up the path and shouted through the open door “Hi, we got the house, and I promised you a bottle if God gave it to us”. She looked at Jane, “What the f**k, you are taking the p***”. “No, we are moving in next week”.

Taking a step back, she shouted back into the house, “they got that f****** house, how mad is that!”

Thankfully, our church was hosting a group of students from the USA at the time. They came every year to do mission work in the area and were quite eager to help, and soon the house would be filled with young students, painting and cleaning.

Much of our belongings were still in storage in the south, and through a friend we arranged a van to bring them north. Another long trip down the M1, this time in an old Transit van. I travelled with our friend, leaving Jane at home to finish the final touches on the house. After 12 hours on the road, we finally arrived back on Banks Road, a round trip in a day. It didn't take long to unload the van and, once done, it was dropped off back in the town to pick up my car. Exhausted and eyes hurting, I drove myself up to our new home. Once parked, I walked in to find Jane finishing the kitchen and preparing a much-needed meal. Realising I had left my jacket in the car, I wandered back to collect it. Getting closer I could see the driver's side window open, closer still I realised it wasn't open, but smashed. Walking around to the driver's door I looked in horror at the car. Four neat holes down the side, window shattered. It didn't take a detective to realise that these were bullet holes. Looking at the car, four hooded characters walked towards me, "Welcome to the Banks, you won't be here long".

In the seconds that followed I had a choice to make, call the police or say nothing. God had called us here for a reason and it could all be over in an instant. Indeed, we wouldn't be here long. I had not seen the culprit, nobody was going to jump to our aid and reporting this now was going to lead to nothing. I walked back into the house and called Jane. She walked out looked at the car in the same way I had, "shine a light!", "just take the car to Colin, it will be safe on his drive tonight".

I drove to Colin, a friend from church, and left the car on his drive. Colin was away and explanations wouldn't be needed to explain how my car had bullet holes in it.

Already completely exhausted, I walked home, the voices of the lads in my mind, "you won't be here long". My heart sank, how I could allow either of us to live like this. I walked through the door and found Jane. The kitchen still smelling of fresh paint, and a microwaved curry. "What are we going to do", "Get the car fixed first thing tomorrow", "well yes", I said, "but what about the lads?" "There's not a lot we can do, we can't leave". Jane was right, we were here, and we needed to show that we were here to help. The following morning, I took the car to the garage and had the window replaced and hoped the holes would not be noticed, they weren't.

A little filler, a touch up paint and a few hours later, no one would know what had happened. We told our new neighbour; her response made us laugh. "It's just a test", you will be ok.

Days and weeks went past and the worry of an impending mob of angry local lads never materialised. We had met both new neighbours and the initial worries had started to disappear.

Chapter 13- Job Centre

Sadly, my days of driving my little Jiffy van were coming to an end. As quickly as I was taken on, I was told they couldn't keep me. Times were hard and selling sandwiches and lunches was a competitive job. My round just wasn't making the money the company needed, and I was let go. We now had rent to pay and all the other bills that went with it.

"I'm going to have to sign on", I said to Jane one morning as we were having breakfast. "It's the last thing I want to do but we won't be able to pay the rent if I don't".

Later that morning, I found myself walking through the door of the local Job Centre. Two large security guards greeted me, they didn't look too dissimilar the night club bouncers I had met while a Street Pastor. These guys however, were far from welcoming, "Do you have an appointment"? "No" I said, slightly taken aback at their rather dominant presence, I want to make a claim, "take a number and sit over there".

Doing as I was told; I walked over to what looked like a parking meter and took a ticket. 353, I looked up at a large screen on the wall, 226. This was going to be a long wait and so I settled back on my hard plastic chair and waited. As I glanced around, taking in the sights, people streamed through the door, greeted by the same angry guards. A girl arrived with her two children. One of the security guys turned to the other, "Oh look, she's brought the kids for a day out", the girl was clearly embarrassed, but the guards just laughed sarcastically and pointed her to the waiting area. Others arrived and wandered off to other areas, while some were aimlessly looking at the various notice boards. An air of desperation filled the space. Rows of desks to the side of the room were filled with staff interviewing downcast faces, faces with a look of despair.

The words of my old pastor in my head, "Will you just be part of the problem?" Here I was, clearly part of the problem. Unemployed and no money. Yet, in this wretched environment, I knew that I had one thing many others didn't have, hope.

I spent the next hour watching the comings and goings, stern officials sitting at desks trying to be helpful as others continued to stream through the door. The occasional shout from an angry "customer" shattered the air "I need my money", shouts that would invariably bring a security guard to keep the peace.

By the time my number flashed up on the screen I was in a daze and jumped out of my seat to avoid going back to the start of the waiting process.

Taking my place on what was now a soft seat with the flashing of orange stuffing leaking at the sides, I was greeted by "Mrs K Smith", my Job Coach.

After what seemed like an eternity of questions, name, age, NI number, address, previous address and inside leg measurements, I had completed the claim part of my visit.

"In order that your claim can proceed you will need to prove you are looking for work, no proof - no money". Her insensitive and rather overbearing manner made me feel like I was back at school. I was presented with a card on which I would record what jobs I had applied for. Over the next two weeks I was told I needed to apply for 21 jobs. If the job centre were not satisfied, I could be sanctioned. It became clear very quickly how the system was working against so many people. I was asked to take a seat again while other forms were gathered for me to take away. Sitting next to me was a young lad, in his twenties, bright blue tracksuit and trainers. "Just blag it mate, I make it up all the time". He was surprisingly chatty and was fidgeting up and down. His name was called and he almost jumped out of his seat, swaggering over to a desk, swinging his cap in his hand he took his papers and headed to the door. "See you Laters" he smirked to the guards on the door, and he was gone. My name was then called, no swagger for me, I politely took my forms and made my way home. I knew after this visit that I wanted to bring some hope into these faces I had seen. I very quickly realised that I would need to muster some hope of my own as I began the task of finding my own job. The town was a very different place from the glory days of steel and coal. Industry was disappearing and jobs were hard to come by. The new government were entering a time of austerity and towns such as this were bearing the brunt. I quickly realised how hard applying for 20 jobs was going to be. Each week I would send off many CVs, make calls and do my best to find work. How easy would it be to throw in the towel and return to the south with our tail between our legs? Each visit to the Job Centre became more demeaning and the condescending attitude of the staff made me feel worthless. The inspection of my job search card was tedious, and I could understand why the young lad had told me to "Just blag it". I was never really asked for evidence and the whole process, as far as I could see, was to make me feel even more worthless.

We had now started to make friends on the estate and Jane had become an unofficial child minder for kids after school. Those that did work had problems with childcare and the lack of facilities made this even worse. Community centres were shut, Sure Start centres had their funding cut, all in the name of this new word, austerity. One evening one of neighbours came knocking at the door. "They've stopped my money, I don't know what to do, can you help?" I had no money to offer, only what little I knew about this new system I was navigating for myself. "I've been told I can appeal, but what does that f***ing mean?" The anger and stress were overpowering and my heart just broke.

The next day I helped to fill out the form and agreed to go into the Job Centre with them. My two new friends on the door made it very clear that only one person could see an adviser and I was told to leave. I kept my cool and calmly told them that people can have support if they wish, my soft southern accent and air of newfound authority seemed to do the trick, and they allowed me in. When our turn arrived, we both went forward to hand in the form and question the adviser. "Who are you?" The adviser was less than pleased to see me, "I'm here as support"." Who do you work for?" "I'm here as support - I don't need to work for anyone". This clearly made the adviser angrier, and I was told the security would remove me if I stayed. Not wanting to put my friend in any more difficulty, I left and was ushered to wait outside. This visit would prove to be the start of something new.

Chapter 14- Meanwhile on the Banks

We had now made new friends and knew that we would need to meet more people. "Why don't we have an open house day?" Jane piped up one morning over breakfast. "Yes, that is a good idea", I said quite confidently.

After a quick chat with our new neighbour, Jane set about organising some food and drinks. We decided that a Saturday would work well and set about inviting people we had met. I made a sign to go on the porch, "OPEN HOUSE, ALL WELCOME".

During the morning, several people came along, and we spent time chatting and telling them of our plans. The doorbell rang and Jane and I went along to welcome our next guest. Standing at the door was a man in his mid-thirties, over six feet tall and very well built. His face was menacing. "What are you doing?" He was clearly not happy. Jane smiled, we're having an open house, and you are welcome to come in. "You better not have pedo's coming in here". We were both taken back and, for a moment, completely speechless. "If you do let them in, I'll have you out of here in an hour".

Jane smiled softly, "That's not what we mean, we just want to help, and we want our home to be your home - we are here to help". The guy looked surprised at Jane, her confidence and warm nature seemed to do the trick. "Well just remember what I've said, I am watching you".

“What’s your name?” Jane asked softly. I’m Terry, I live just around the corner. “I’m Nige, this is Jane, we are Christians, and we hope we can help”.

Inwardly, we were both completely trembling at this tower of a man at our door. Why he thought open house would mean what he thought had really shaken us. Terry turned and walked away. Going back into the kitchen we just looked at each other, no words needed.

“You make sure you keep him on side”, Marie had clearly overheard his voice, “he’s not messing, he will have you shot out if he doesn’t like you”. The reality of estate life was becoming clear and building trust was not going to be easy.

Marie, was our new friend, she lived just across the road and was the other half of the two girls we had met on the kerb before moving in. She was tough, very tough. Born and brought up on the estate, she knew everyone and everyone knew her. She lived in a house with two boys aged six and seven. Her down-to-earth attitude and constant clichés led me to warm to her very quickly. ” I’m clamming me, me stomachs eating me back”, to name one of many. [*Clamming, Hungry!]

Marie had seemed to warm to us, and we knew quickly that her insight into the community was going to be invaluable. We had learned in our time in Oxford that we needed a “King Pin”. Just like in bowling, you hit the king pin and the rest will fall. Marie was going to be our king pin. It was not difficult to like her, she was grounded, raw and had a strong sense of right from wrong. She understood the language of the streets and was quick to point out what people thought about life on the estate and in the town. "Why would Terry be thinking we wanted sex offenders in our house?" I asked quite startled. "Terry just thinks open house means anyone can come and that could mean pedos". Marie's matter of fact points left us in a state of shock. We really needed to understand the culture of this place. To our relief, Marie did speak to Terry and when I saw him in the street, he would nod his head in a vague but rather menacing acknowledgement.

The day of the open house had been a great opportunity to hear from the local folk what was needed. Finding something for the kids to do was difficult and local provision had been cut. It became the norm for our new neighbours to ask if we could look after the kids for an hour. Our new home and its large kitchen soon became the home to various arts, crafts and games. The house did indeed become an open one and it was quite normal for people to open the door, shout and just come in. I laugh when I think I could be sat on the sofa and hear a voice shout through "Only me"! The door would fly open and in they would come. "Hey, look after Tracey for an hour, will you?"

This wasn't formal, these folks had become friends and with it brought a valuable trust.

As time went by, we continued to walk and pray around the estate. It was one such day that we were walking with friends from church. We often paused at the school and community centre. There we would pray and ask God's blessing. Across from the community centre was the Methodist Church, again we would pause and pray.

The Methodist Church had been built at the same time as the estate, it was quite a foreboding building and had clearly seen better days. As we paused, a tall well-built man approached us. He had a big smile and immediately I thought he looked like a gentle giant. "Hello, what are you doing?" he asked inquisitively, we explained that we prayed around the estate and introduced ourselves. "What a great idea, why don't we do that?" I must have looked quite puzzled at his response, I laughed, and said, "I don't know, but you are welcome to join us". He smiled, "I will let people know". We exchanged details and he wandered back into the building.

A week later, Bob, his wife Jilly, and some others from the church joined us as we walked the estate. Bob had been a head teacher before retiring and was a keen rugby player in his day. That was no surprise, and I did think he would have been a formidable figure to meet on the field. He was indeed a gentle giant. We talked and prayed together, sharing some of our thoughts and visions for the estate.

It became apparent that the church really had a heart for the area but for many reasons had not made the impact they wanted. It was an aging congregation and had started to dwindle.

We left Bob and walked home, another great encounter and we were pleased to meet such faithful people.

It would be another few weeks before our contact with the church would go to another level.

It was late afternoon, and the sound of knocking came from the front door. Normally the door would fly open and one of the neighbours would walk straight in. Nobody entered and the door knocked again.

I went to the door to see a lady standing on the doorstep. Dressed in a smart black suit and wearing a clerical shirt, she smiled as I opened the door. "Hello, is it Nigel?" "Yes", Jane then appeared from upstairs, "this is Jane".

I am Rosemary, Minister from the Methodist Church. We invited her through, and she explained that she had heard about our prayer walk. Sitting with coffee we began to explain what we were doing and spoke of our vision for the estate. Rosemary quickly understood and seemed pleased that we had made contact. "Bob was telling me about your walk, he was actually quite cross that we hadn't thought of praying around the estate" We just laughed.

Rosemary listened and her response was going to help us take our vision to a new level.

“You must find it a little cramped in here, if you would like the use of a room at the church, you would be welcome”. Jane and I knew that it wasn’t ideal that our kitchen had become a mini kids club, and going forward would be increasingly difficult. “That would be amazing, we said at almost the same time. We arranged to meet Rosemary at the church later in the week.

Chapter 15- ASSIST & Doctor Who

Though things had started to move forward, we were still trying to make ends meet for ourselves. I really needed a proper income, and jobs were scarce. I had to find something that would enable me to be in the community and at the same time keep us financially stable. This was going to be no easy task.

My last visit to the Job Centre had planted a seed in my mind. I had been told in no uncertain terms I was not welcome when I went along with a friend. I wanted to help but the way in which the centre worked was against me.

So many people were struggling with a system that was either broken or unreachable. So many people didn't have the education that I had been gifted. I knew the language of authority and would not be bullied into situations that were put there to prevent people getting the help they desperately needed.

If I was unable to get a job, I would work for the Lord in a new way. A Bible verse rang through my ears, "speak up for those who cannot speak for themselves".

After some time of prayer, an idea came to me. I decided to become an advocate, someone who could help people with forms, benefits, and appeals. A sort of mobile citizen's advice bureau. Though the town did have a Citizens Advice, it wasn't always possible to get an appointment quickly and the wait times, when you did get in, were long.

I had navigated the benefit system for myself and had seen a way that I could help others. At the time, the Job Centres were advertising opportunities for business start-ups. I had no intention of starting a business as such but could see a way to use this to my advantage.

If I become self-employed, I would be eligible for grants and could also claim tax credits.

Within a month I had started the plans and returned to the Job Centre to close my claim. My appointment with Mrs Smith was very different, quite simply because I was out of her hair, someone else's problem. "Well Mr Perrott, I really hope it goes well, and we don't want to see you again, do we?"

Her condescending voice required a huge amount of grace. I almost felt as though I was being released from prison. I smiled through gritted teeth and went on my way.

She would have no idea that she would indeed see me again, in a very different role.

It wasn't too long before I was indeed back at the Job Centre, this time with another friend. The words of the adviser when I had tried to help before rang in my head "who do you work for?" I could hardly say Jesus, the thought had occurred to me but though true, it would have brought my friends from the door even more quickly. It was then that I recalled "Doctor Who", I am a big fan. The Doctor always carried a little wallet with a blank white card inside. Whoever the Doctor flashed the card to, would see whatever he wanted them to see. It was some kind of mind-bending trick.

One evening I set about making my own ID card. My name, title: Advocate, etc. A nice plastic holder and a lanyard purchased from the internet. There was nothing untrue in anything I included, I was indeed an advocate and had a little non-profit business called ASSIST.

Sporting my new lanyard, I entered the Job Centre with my new friend, they were never clients. As suspected, I was challenged, flashed my "white card" and I was in. It was for me, a David and Goliath moment. I was indeed going in the name of the Lord God Almighty.

Walking over to the desk, I took a chair and placed it alongside the other. The face of Mrs K Smith was one of utter disdain as I took my seat, and I was quietly rather enjoying the moment.

I sat next to my friend and helped to navigate the questions. I believe Mrs Smith started to realise that my presence helped them both.

The next month or so brought a new determination and several phone calls, emails, meetings and trolling the internet started to pay off.

I had, by this time, managed to make new friends and was put in touch with a local funding body. They gave grants to new Christian projects, and I managed to secure £5000 start up. At the same time "Christians Against Poverty" (CAP) were also employing new debt coaches. The role involved meeting people in their homes, helping them with budgets and gathering information that CAP would use to help them either pay their debts off or get them to a more manageable state. Getting through someone's front door in the name of Jesus made me smile. CAP is unashamedly Christian and their calling to reach those people who were at their wits end was right up my street. It was simple, we brought the hope that so many people needed, into some very dark places. As a paid role and alongside my advocacy role, things were starting to fall into place.

It didn't take long for people on the estate to hear that I wanted to help - everything from passport forms to housing benefit. At CAP, I seized numerous training opportunities, attending as many benefits' awareness courses as possible. The system was complicated, and my heart always went out to people who just found the whole process stressful.

The government of the day were trying to save money, and the benefit bill was always a good place to start. Sanctions were coming thick and fast and it always felt like I was going into battle when another appeal form landed in front of me.

Mick had been on drugs and after several prison holidays finally found himself clean from his addictions. I had visited Mick through CAP. His debts were not too serious and unlike the many others I had seen, I knew we could help quite quickly. I arrived at his hostel one morning. It was a new build, not that dissimilar to a hotel from the outside. One side of the building housed new folk, sometimes straight off the street, the other side was known as "move on", it was for the more established residents who had their own room and were able to access support for jobs and more permanent accommodation. Mick was in "Move on" and was not in his usual good mood, when I arrived in reception to meet him. "They have stopped my f***ing money, I've missed an appointment, and I didn't even know". Mick was a spindly character and was missing his front teeth. Spitting out the language that I was now was quite comfortable with, he thrust a crumbled-up piece of brown paper into my hand, a letter from the benefits office.

Dear Mr M,

Non-Attendance

You have breached your job seekers agreement, and a sanction has been applied to your account.

The letter went on to explain that a sanction of six weeks had been applied, and a lower rate of benefit would now apply. "They didn't tell me, I never got nothing". Mick was clearly distraught.

Recent visits to the Job Centre had taught me that going to complain would be fruitless and in most cases the security guards would escort the angry protesters from the building. "Fill out the appeal form".

Most wouldn't bother and would find other ways to find an income. "Ok, Mick let's sort this". It was never a quick process, and his money would have been reinstated by the time we got an appeal. There was a principle here too - Mick wanted affirmation that he was telling the truth and should not be punished in this way.

When appeals were heard, it generally took place at the Magistrate's Court. Mick's appeal arrived, most never attended, but today Mick was with me. Entering the court, I unloaded my briefcase case into the scanner, arms in the air, I walked through the security gate. A cheery security chap gave me a big smile. Mick on the other hand was handled differently, "take your cap off, keys, phone and money in the tray".

Finally, into the waiting area, we took our seats and waited to be called into the court, which was a large room with what looked an oversized dining table. A judge, a clerk and a representative from the

Department of Work and Pensions. The process is short and the DWP are usually in a hurry to move from case to case. The rep was clearly surprised that Mick had arrived in person and more surprised that he was represented. As I was not a solicitor, I had to ask the judge for permission to support my friend. The judge, a lady of middle age, asked my name and role. My plastic badge was not going to cut it here and I had to explain my role in the community. Inwardly, I was shaking and hoping I wasn't going to be thrown out or arrested. To my surprise the judge gave me a warm smile, "admirable that you want to help".

The case was duly read out, "failure to attend appointments, leading to six weeks sanction".

"We wrote to Mr M on the 18th of July inviting him for an interview on 26th July. This is the second time he failed to attend". Mick became angry and I placed my hand on his arm to prevent an outburst.

The DWP had not known that Mick lived in a managed hostel. All mail coming into the building came through reception, it was noted and held. On collection, the mail was signed for. DWP letters are always noted for this reason. Mick was able to prove that no letters had been received during the timescale they had suggested. "Well, this is nice and simple, appeal, "approved" the judge smiled and we left the room. I must say the look on the DWP officer's face was worth the visit. Mick was exonerated and his money backdated.

Mick was over the moon, and inwardly I was praising God for yet another David and Goliath moment. Having to go into a court like a criminal to appeal something that was rightfully theirs was a moment where I could actually "speak up".

I attended the court for many others, often in front of the same judge, a judge who I eventually realised was as appalled by the callous nature of the DWP, as I was. I never lost an appeal.

So many problems: debt, unemployment and addiction, the town had many different groups involved in these issues. It was good to work alongside so many different agencies. It didn't take long to see a big hole in these services. Food, a town of this size that didn't have a coordinated Foodbank. What did people do if they were sanctioned or had an emergency. I was one person, I clearly could not meet the need on my own, not even with Jane, our secret weapon. Our estate was really in need, and I knew I had to act.

The Food Bank

I had helped at the food bank in our last town and quickly decided that we would need to do something similar here. I approached our church and quickly the idea caught on. Through other church contacts I began to get more and more support. I contacted the food bank network, and a representative came to talk to us. It took some time to get the red tape out of the way. Convincing churches that they would need to help financially was the most difficult. It became apparent very quickly that a foodbank on The Banks was never going to be enough, so many areas of the town were struggling. This brought more churches and more importantly, more volunteers. Newsletters and publicity followed and our very first food collection was arranged. We had been gifted an old disused church hall from the Anglican Church, and this would be our new storage hub. Our first collection of food arrived at the hall, four banana boxes, stuffed with long life milk, cans and packets. It really didn't take long before the word got out and the community spirit took over. Tons of food donated via supermarket collections, local businesses and trade unions poured into our hub. Six satellite hubs were created around the town and within a year, food was being distributed five days a week. The many agencies, and others, distributed vouchers to their clients. As the bank grew, so did the workload. I was now being paid a day a week to manage the operation. The local council decided to give a large grant to what had now become a registered charity. The first year would see over 5000 food parcels given, in the years that followed this number would treble.

In just over two years, I had become part of the problem and was now part of the solution, working alongside many others bringing some much-needed hope to a desperate community.

I remembered sitting in that chair on that Sunday morning, "Ok, I want to serve you". Yet, in all that was being achieved, there was still something in my heart that said I needed to do more, but what?

Chapter 16- TFFC – The Family Friendly Centre

It was a Thursday afternoon, and this was the day we had arranged to meet Rosemary. The church was a short walk from our house. We had walked past the building many times but apart from a pause to pray for them, we really didn't take much notice.

The church had been built in the '50s and was not the most attractive of buildings. It was set back from the road, with a large car park in front. To one side was a small hall, connected to the main church building via a U-shaped red brick corridor. The main church itself was a formidable building, with the same-coloured bricks. The high roof towered over the terrace houses alongside. The large arched front door was hidden behind a padlocked wrought iron gate. Drainpipes and the flat roof had barbed wire with anti-graffiti paint, clearly fitted to prevent the inevitable climbers from gaining access. External windows were fitted with plastic opaque glass that again would stop stones or missiles getting through. The car park's old tarmac was full of potholes and crunched beneath our feet as we walked to the side door. The light behind the plastic window, and the solitary car in the car park, indicated someone was in the building.

The old wooden door in the centre of the corridor opened easily and we stepped inside. A sign in front of us indicated left to the halls and right for the church. Just as we began to decide which way to turn, Rosemary appeared from the left. Her cheery voice welcomed us, and she eagerly came to greet us, “Come on through, I’ll show you our halls”. The slightly off pink walls were complemented with red and grey lino floor tiles. I whispered to Jane, it does look like something out of the ’50s”. We followed down the narrow corridor, which had various storage areas behind closed doors and entered a large airy hall, which wasn’t visible from the outside and the huge expanse came as a shock. The large wooden floor was marked with various lines - football, and badminton were clearly played in this hall. To the left was a large stage with dark red curtains draped on either side. To one side, there was a serving hatch that led through to a large kitchen. It was enormous and though clearly dated, it was an impressive space. The proximity to the kitchen made it a great space for serving meals and drinks.

Rosemary explained that, indeed, various games were played, and the hall was used by many groups including a local theatre group and the Scouts.

Coming out of the main hall, we were led into another hall, smaller than the first, but still a good space. This was the room seen from the outside and, before the main church had been built, had served as the church. Through another door and yet another small hall appeared. As we entered, we immediately knew what the room was used for. It looked like any primary school classroom and the various Bible pictures and books told us this was the Sunday school room. The last room we came to was piled up with boxes, an old desk in the corner and bright yellow 1970's curtains hung from the windows. The tatty carpet had long given up and various areas were held down with black tape. "This was the old Vestry". It was still used to count the money from the Sunday services but was clearly not a usable space. The sheer size of this building took our breath away.

Though still used by a variety of groups it had certainly seen its day. This once busy place was now a shadow of its heyday. Returning down the corridor we entered the rear of the church. Another huge space with a very high ceiling. To our surprise, the pews had long since been removed and comfy chairs had taken their place. This was another usable space, and it clearly had loads of potential.

Rosemary explained that the congregation had dwindled, and they were thinking about demolishing the church, selling the land and retreating to the smaller hall for their worship. An architect's plan on the wall in the foyer showed three houses built on the plot. This was clearly a topic of much conversation with the members.

Our own thoughts were that of horror that this amazing space could be torn down, but we kept our thoughts to ourselves. We were really impressed with the spaces available and knew that we could hold some great groups there. Returning home, Jane was full of ideas of all the ways we could use the building and we both felt a sense of excitement.

That evening, Marie came over to see us and we chatted about the visit to the church. Marie was less than impressed, apparently, they were snobs and wanted nothing to do with the people on the estate. Most of the kids would use the building as a climbing frame and take great delight in terrorising the congregation and visitors to the building. We had also learned on our brief visit that the church had a volunteer who would sit in their car on a Sunday morning to keep an eye on the parked vehicles, and the barbed wire and plastic windows had now started to make sense.

We talked with Marie about some of the needs we had seen so far and asked her what she thought.

"We need a breakfast club" Some people that worked could not afford pre-school childcare and the school itself had no provision for it. We already had several kids that would come along to the house after school and the idea of having them from early morning was clearly not going to work. This new opportunity of using the church came exactly at the right time.

Chapter 17 - A Strain in the Relationship

The call to the North was firmly being affirmed in our hearts and living on the estate had become our focus and more importantly we had grown a heart connection to the people. Life was tough for so many, and we both knew this was not going to be easy.

We were part of a church that had welcomed us, and they seemed to want us to succeed. We felt at home on a Sunday morning and had made friends. The CAP office was based at the church, and I would use a room for some of my Foodbank and ASSIST business.

By this stage Jane and I had gathered a small bunch of children who would eagerly join in some of our activities, and the leadership team felt they needed to be integrated into the life of the church.

This was going to prove difficult as the kids on the Banks were not usually that well behaved and though the services were very informal, they would struggle to fit in. The church was a bus ride into the town centre and though many of the kids were used to bus rides, their behaviour, shall we say, was usually a little erratic.

After a few confrontations with bus drivers, and angry passengers we felt another option was needed and the Sunday visits came to an end.

Though there was always enthusiasm for what we were doing, the zeal often disappeared when we asked the question, "Who would like to help us?"

As the months passed by, we began to put on a few smaller events at the church on the estate. This had led to the idea of some joint Sunday services between the

Methodists and our church. If the kids and families could not get into town, then the church should come to them. Though in principle this sounded like a good idea, Jane and I were not that comfortable with the idea. Things we had learned from our time in Oxford told us not to jump too quickly.

As we sat in our kitchen on the morning of this special service we felt a sense of trepidation. "Do you think anyone will actually come from the estate"? Jane was looking worried. "I really don't know love, I'm not really sure they are ready" Jane smiled, "who the Methodists, or our lot?" I laughed, "Everyone, I think!"

The Methodist church had a weekly service at 9.30am on a Sunday morning and our church met at 10.30am in the town centre. We decided that we would hold something at 11am and invite people along who might like to try something different. It was felt that the service should take place in the large hall rather than the church as it was less foreboding and more informal. Setting up a service took time, there were speakers, microphones and a band all to be readied. As Jane and I arrived, we were greeted with cables, sound desk and a few eager volunteers from our church. My mind went back to the time I first arrived in that school hall. Would this have the same impact on those arriving today? Something inside me told me, no.

As we continued to prepare the space, the distant sound of the organ and traditional hymn singing echoed down the corridor from the main church. Their service was coming to an end, and we would soon be joined by the congregation for coffee. Bob and Jilly were the first to arrive, their smiling faces were a joy to see. Whatever the circumstances, they always smiled and greeted everyone with warmth. Slowly, more arrived, their smart Sunday suits in contrast to the informal look of our group. Pleasantries were exchanged, coffee was consumed, and the atmosphere felt relaxed. Slowly people began to disappear and only a handful of people from the earlier service remained. Undeterred, the service began with enthusiastic worship, music brought by our visiting musicians. As we gazed around the large hall, we soon realised that nobody from the estate had joined us, but at that moment, the large door of the hall banged open, and three kids from the community came bounding in. Their loud giggles of excitement and constant chatter made their presence well felt. It didn't take long for faces to be turned, looking at Jane and I to control these loud and brash kids. To my surprise, the first sound of "shush" didn't come from the hosts but from one of our group. "You need to sit down". These kids were less than worried about being told off and the more distain from the congregation brought more giggles and fidgeting. The service continued and by the close, we both felt a sense of relief that it was over. As the band and volunteers began to clear away, the kids became more animated and were running up and down the corridor making their presence well known. They certainly took delight in making fun of people and generally misbehaving. At this point, one of the elders of our church approached Jane with a face of thunder. "Will you please control these kids". "Jane was shocked at his outburst, "I am sorry, but this is why we are here, we love these kids". His faced turned red with anger and as he walked away, he said, "well you f**ing look after them then". Jane was stunned and was left standing in silence at what she had just heard.

Walking slowly home, Jane was clearly upset, "How could he speak to me like that?" I too felt hurt. The words I had heard years before, "I will do the judging". It was this kind of hypocrisy that had forced me away from the church. How could I remain in an organisation that proclaimed love and yet lived with so much anger and impatience?

The significance of this morning was a culmination of many weeks of misunderstanding of what we both felt we had been called to do. Jane had said that morning, "we love these kids" this was so true. In the short time we had lived in this community we had started to get an understanding of who they were and the lives they lived. It was becoming clear that not only would we have a great deal of trust to forge within the community, but we would also have to navigate the different personalities within the church at the same time.

Jane and I spent an evening praying and talking over the difficulties we were facing. The disaster of the morning service and the control and direction our church felt we should be taking. We decided we needed to meet with one of the elders and talk through how we felt things were going. I phoned the Pastor, explained what had happened, and we arranged to meet later in the week.

The afternoon arrived and we sat in our living room with coffee and cake. The light conversation soon turned to the matter in hand. The Pastor smiled and spoke softly, "I have spoken with George, and he tells me that you must have misheard him". Jane laughed, "I know exactly what he said, and I certainly didn't mishear him".

Again, the Pastor smiled, “Jane, this is not first time you have got people wrong” Jane was looking puzzled by his response,” and what does that mean?” Again, he tried to be calm, “People want to help and sometimes, when they don’t act in the way you think they should, you get annoyed. “I get annoyed when people treat others badly or have a different agenda”. It was the Pastor’s turn to look puzzled, “I’m not sure what you mean, Jane”. It was at this point I felt I needed to step in. I was annoyed and did my best to keep my cool. “We are trying to make relationships; we live here, and the people are becoming our friends”. I explained that words spoken wrongly can have bad repercussions, not only for us but those around us, the very people we want to serve. The inner annoyance I had for church was beginning to rise again and I had to muster a great deal of grace to deal with the situation.

It was clear that my frustration was going nowhere, and the conversation became more difficult. “Look, “we know people want to help, but just turning up and being around is not enough, constantly telling the kids off when they are overexcited is not help”. I was referring to some of the events that we had started to put on, including a recent jumble sale.

A couple of local families had suggested that an indoor car boot sale would be a good idea, and it would help local people. We never dismissed an idea that came from the community and jumped at the opportunity. Having sought permission from the Methodist Church we had the use of their large hall for a morning. We then arranged for some help from our church and volunteers stepped up. Though we were grateful for the support, it didn’t take long for some regret to arise.

Cadey and Leigh arrived early, pushing their bits and bobs around to the church in an old pram. To be greeted by these two girls, with beaming smiles, was so much fun. These girls were still at the local primary school but were happily trusted by their mum to make the short walk to the church on their own. A few minutes later, others would arrive, carrying and pushing the various things they hoped to sell or swap. We were really looking forward to meeting some new people and seeing the church open and ready for local people to arrive felt fantastic.

Our first volunteer appeared not long after and they agreed to help in the kitchen. Annie was pleasant and had been a part of our church for a few years. After setting up kettles and sorting the kitchen, she made her way into the main hall. On seeing the girls set out their wares, Annie began questioning. "Where are your parents", "Our mam is working this morning". Annie looking perplexed continued, "You shouldn't be here on your own".

On hearing the conversation, I stepped in. "It's ok, we know mum, and it's fine". Annie was clearly in confusion and wanted more information. "What about their dad?" Smiling and doing my best to keep my frustration inside, I explained. "They don't have a dad around at the moment; mum is single and is happy for them to be here on their own. What Annie had not known was that dad was in prison at the time. Annie, clearly not happy, turned and made her way back to the kitchen. The girls, though young, were so much older than their years laughed, and Cadey smirking, said, "Oh get the clip of her". I did my best not to laugh and moved away. The morning brought lots of people through the door, and it didn't take long before it became obvious that the two girls were well known to the community. Though mum was not present, other mums, aunties and uncles, as they were often known, were looking out for them.

The morning came and went, and we both felt the time had been successful. The girls were the last to leave and we said our goodbyes. That afternoon, Jane and I were sat in the kitchen and the door knocked. Cadey and Leighs mums, standing on the doorstep. Smiling, Jane opened the door. Her face didn't look happy, "Who was that woman who shouted at my kids?" "It's a good job I wasn't there cos she would be on her back".

Jane was stunned, "I am so sorry, "I" ... Before Jane could finish, mum continued, "tell her from me, keep her nose out of my business" she turned and was gone before any more explanations could be made. Walking back into the kitchen, Jane was clearly devastated, we both sat with our heads in our hands. A few short words, said in a moment had caused such distress.

Sitting with the Pastor, I told the story and gave other examples of where good intentions had been taken very badly. We were still strangers to many people and the trust needed for us to build strong relationships was still a long way off. I went on to explain that we didn't think that running a Sunday service at this time was a good idea, the people were not ready, not only the locals but also the church. I went on to talk about the launch of our breakfast club and the Pastors response took me by surprise. "If we can't hold a Sunday service and get the kids to behave, then a breakfast club has to be out of the question" Jane and I were less than happy with his response. "Sorry Guys, we don't want you to do anymore at the moment, we can look at this again in the future".

"So, we have to stop all the work we have started?" I was now in dismay. "Guys, the elders feel that you are getting this wrong".

We had both been in this position before, being told we were wrong, and we couldn't do what we felt God was calling us to. I was a great deal stronger than in the past, what we had already experienced told us we needed to press on. "I am so sorry, but we cannot stop, and if the church doesn't support us, then sadly we will need to go it alone". The Pastor became a little flustered at our intentions. "If you want to leave the church that's ok, but what about your role in the Foodbank?" "What do you mean?" I asked. "Well, you started the Foodbank through our church, if you leave, you won't be able to continue".

I was now annoyed; I had indeed started the Foodbank while at the church but had ensured that it was not owned by any one church. I had gathered several other churches and recruited trustees to form a charity. The constitution clearly stated that the Foodbank was an ecumenical charity, and I was employed by that charity. I calmly explained this and reinforced our intention to leave the church. The Pastor, clearly exasperated at our determination to continue, said his goodbyes and left.

I felt frustrated but with a sense of purpose I rang and made an appointment to meet an Anglican colleague to get further advice. I explained our situation and he agreed that my paid role for the Foodbank was never in question and the other trustees would support me.

In all our frustrations and annoyance with people who we felt did not understand us, we also knew we could not do this on our own. Our options for support were limited and we were still so new to this northern town.

Chapter 18 - Breakfast

It was 6am when the alarm went off and I wasn't feeling any enthusiasm to get out of bed. I staggered down the stairs, put the kettle on and stared out of the window into the darkness of our back garden. Marie had insisted that this was a good idea and though we agreed enthusiastically, inwardly we both felt a sense of foreboding. The night before we had been in the hall, setting out a toaster, getting tables ready and chatted about what we could do if kids arrived. Marie had told us that we needed Coco Pops and Nutella. Not the healthiest option but we already knew that dietary requirements were not high on the kids' agendas.

Of course, Jilly and Bob had agreed to help, and by the time we reached the church, the lights were on, and they were both in the kitchen. Bob sporting his Union Jack apron and Jilly in her Cath Kidston floral attire.

Even at this early hour, their smiles and warmth shone through, "Would you like coffee?" Jane was quick to reply, "Yes, a bucket please".

We had already set up and now needed to wait for the imminent arrival of kids. It would be another 40 minutes before Marie arrived with her two boys. They were clearly unimpressed to be there but on the command of mam, had finally got out of bed.

We decided on just one day a week, getting up early was going to be tough and we knew volunteers were going to be difficult to find. We sat and played a couple of table games and munched on some toast. The hour flew by, and Jane and I agreed to walk the boys over the road. The school was just a few steps away so within a couple of minutes we found ourselves in the playground as the boys ran off to find friends. We knew some faces and Jane was quick to start up a conversation with a mum. "We've started a breakfast club", mum was quick with her response, "How much in for the kids?", "Just a pound lovey", Jane responded. We hadn't decided on any price, and I laughed with Jane later about how she had plucked a figure out of the sky. "It's not about the money is it" Jane said. No love it's not, and it's more important that people know we're here".

The following morning our new mum arrived and handed over her son. With Jane making more friends in the playground and Marie helping to get the word out, more kids would arrive. Each morning, we would play a couple of games and sit and chat with the few kids that would come along. It wasn't long before we were asked the dreaded question, "Why don't do you do more days?" We knew that we would eventually have to increase the days as more kids started to attend. Bob and Jilly agreed to do one other day and another lady from church agreed to help. So, a second day started, and more kids began to attend. Within months, our table games had grown to team games with over fifteen kids in each team. We were now doing four days a week, and the filing cabinet was filling with more and more consent forms.

It was around this time we received a call from a local housing officer. Much of the estate was owned by a social housing provider, and they were keen to see the area improved. Janet was involved in community engagement and word of our breakfast club had reached her. She asked if her and a colleague could drop in and see what we were up to. I was more than happy to make contact, and we invited her along the following week.

Monday morning was always a difficult one, the kids had generally been up late over the weekend, and they were less than happy to be dragged out of bed. Starting this new week would not be any different and by the time Janet arrived with her colleague the club was in full swing. A smell of toast and kids tucking into their Nutella while others eagerly ran around wanting to play a game. We immediately took a shine to Janet, for a Monday morning she seemed bright and full of enthusiasm and certainly was not put off by the busyness of the morning. We explained how the mornings ran, and she was keen to chat to the kids. By the end of the session, she had agreed to help walk them to school. "I think this is such a great idea and clearly there is a real need for this, we would really like to support it". We were both quite excited at the prospect and tried our best not to be too eager. "How do you think you may be able to help?" Well firstly, we have funding for community projects, and I would be happy to help you claim it". This was fantastic news and as we knew funding was going to be an issue going forward, and this had come at the right time. Janet went on to explain that her niece attended the school and for two days a week she took her along. "If you like, I will come and help out on the days I have her". This was another answer to prayer, and we quickly accepted her offer. Janet was true to her word and, after applying for funds, we were successful in gaining a grant. By now the club was becoming established and we had 45 kids registered. The walk to school was becoming a military exercise and went generally without incident. Jane's voice would boom out as we lined up before leaving "Get in your pairs, Lindsey stopping pulling Kerry's hair, Stop, I didn't say anyone could go yet". The kids, too, would always have their own issues, “I’m not walking with her, she’s kicked me”, “hey Jane, Tommy just swore”.

By the time we reached the playground it was a relief as the kids would fly off in different directions before the bell would ring. The kids would then form orderly queues with their classmates before being beckoned into the school. We were always amazed at how well they behaved for the teachers and only minutes earlier had caused us mayhem walking up the road. More volunteers would eventually arrive as willing parents stepped up to help.

Munchies breakfast club had arrived, was now well known, and was supported by the community. Our thoughts and prayers quickly turned to what came next.

Chapter 19 - Marie

Marie had unknowingly become our champion, a girl from the estate who had a life story that could be a novel. A tall statue, with an array of tattoos that were as colourful as her personality. She had an ability to see into the hearts of those around her and knew if the attention she received was genuine. The late evangelist, Tony Campolo, once said, “To truly love your neighbour, you need to see Jesus in the heart of the other”. The first time we met Marie, we could see Jesus in her. The time we arrived with a bottle of Lambrini and had sat together in our neighbour’s living room. It was then that she showed herself as vulnerable and yet so strong. She had shared something of her life story and asked a question, a small tear running down her face, “where do you think Jesus was then?” This question couldn’t be answered at the time but would lead to something very powerful as time went on. Her life had been fraught with difficulties, a single parent, bringing up to two young boys wasn’t an easy task. She saw the injustices of life and was quick and vocal at pointing them out. Thankfully for us, Marie saw something in Jane and me and wanted to be a part of what we were trying to do on the estate.

As time went by, we became closer, and I would spend time talking about my faith and how God had come into my life. Marie had a great sense of humour, dry, just like mine. As I shared my own story, we would laugh at my many mistakes and she quickly found out, that I too, could swear almost as well as she could. Sometimes we would end up like kids in a school playground, laughing at the sound a fart makes, or recounting times when we had been sick after a good night out.

Eventually, barriers were removed, and I was able to bring Jesus more formally into our conversations. That person I once was, had gone, though it was my story, it wasn't the end, and it was something I was able to share with this wonderful person.

I knew that Marie needed some space from the daily hustle and bustle of estate life. Each time we met it would always be interrupted by the comings and goings of other people through the door. I needed time to take these conversations to another level. It was then an idea came to me, a weekend away.

A friend from the church had a small cottage In Cumbria, he rented it out as a holiday let and he was more than happy to let me use it for a weekend.

When I asked Marie if she fancied a couple of days away in the country, she was more than happy and said the boys would really enjoy it.
The weekend arrived and we set off after school on the long drive across the Pennines to Cumbria. The boys were clearly happy and as the roads become narrower and tiny villages flashed by. It was almost dark when we arrived, the village had few streetlights, and then, up a narrow-cobbled drive we arrived at what was once an old barn. A large oak door surrounded by grey stone greeted us. As I fumbled with the keys, the door opened into a small hallway, in front was a tiny shower room and then two compact bedrooms. A wooden staircase led up to a large open plan living space and kitchen. The large space had a log burning stove in the centre and several large comfy sofas which turned into beds were set around the room. The boys were now

overexcited, they had never seen anywhere like this. Running up and down the stairs, exploring every cupboard and space. Their attention then turned to the portable TV in the corner of the room. The boys, who were more used to their 60" widescreen had never seen a small portable TV from the '90s. Turning it on, a crackle and white fuzz across the screen, "Sorry boys, the TV doesn't work, there are some video cassettes with films". Eyes open wide, they looked in horror, and said, "You're having a laugh aren't you". "Nope" I smiled. Marie too was laughing, "You're not here for TV".

Slumping on the sofa and knowing that pleading wasn't going to work, the boys turned their attention to the next request. "What's to eat?" This was easier and we unpacked the various things we had brought along. Crisps to start, followed by a lasagne we had made before we left. Later in the evening, Marie settled the boys into the downstairs bedroom, and we sat back with drinks. "What do you think, do you like it here?" Marie was quick to respond, "I love it Nige", thanks to you two for bringing us". Marie had no idea that we had an ulterior motive for bringing her along and I wanted to make the most of this time away. "Marie, I want to ask you a question, not now, but by the time we leave" "yeah, what it is?" She asked looking slightly puzzled. "It is six words" yeah, but what are they?" I smiled, "well, I'm not going to tell you, not yet, I want you to work it out". I laughed and Marie, looking even more inquisitive, had her say, "No, tell me now" I laughed, wait and see. At that, Jane changed the subject, "Who wants a hot chocolate", the moment passed, and we all went off to bed.

The following morning the boys were up early, food always being the first thing asked for. Jane, always on the ball had sorted a full English breakfast. With the smell of bacon cooking and strong coffee, we talked about what we were going to do for the day. “Would you like to explore the village?” It was a cold grey day as we ventured outside. A few stone cottages and a stream running through the centre. We walked up a narrow lane passing a few smaller buildings. One of the cottages had a low stone wall and a well-kept green lawn. In the centre of the garden stood a lovely stone well, complete with bucket and pulley. Before I could open my mouth, the boys had gone, and within seconds, had jumped the wall raced across the garden to see this new sight. “Boys that is someone’s garden! Come away”. A loud tapping on a window and an angry face appeared. Marie, then joined in the frantic beckoning, “Boys get out of that f***ing garden”; laughing and enjoying every moment, the boys came back. Inwardly, I was cringing, but I knew that the boys had not experienced anything like this before and were just exploring in the only way they knew how. Jane, whispered in my ears,” Oh my days”. The only thing we could do was laugh and move on as quickly as we could.

Our walk continued out of the village and onto a small road that ran alongside a large open field. Sheep were quietly grazing, minding their own business, until we arrived! Standing at the gate of the field, Marie began whistling and shouting, “Look I can make the sheep move” clearly delighted at putting this newfound gift into practice, she kept shouting with joy as she saw the sheep move across the field. We continued our walk and finally made our way back. An evening meal followed, and the boys went off to bed.

Conversation then turned to the many questions Marie had about faith, Jesus and the church. Some questions went unanswered but others, though time needed, were explained. It was early morning when I finally got to ask the question. "So, Marie, what have you got to lose?" she was by now, exasperated, "What are the six words?!" I laughed and said again, "what have you got to lose?" By this point she was getting frustrated, and I knew I had to let on. "Love, they are the six words!", "What have you got to lose, I can't answer all your questions, but in the end, the question remains in those six words, what have you got to lose?". Finally, Marie realised what I was saying and laughed. "Ok, I get it!"

I was tired, Jane was tired, and Marie was finally starting to realise what was happening. "I've nothing to lose and really want to know Jesus". In the early hours of the morning, in a barn, in the middle of nowhere, we prayed together. It would be a few days later that this time would conclude.

Back home, the weekend behind us, Marie walked over to see us, and as always bounded through the door, "Only me" Sitting in the kitchen, Jane and I were eating. "What are you having?" she asked. "Just a bit of salmon, would you like some?" She curled her face and laughed, "oh no, I'd rather plait my own snot!" Her little sayings always made us roar with laughter.

Making herself a cup of tea, she sat and began chatting. "I've been thinking about the weekend, what should I do?"

"Do you want to follow Jesus?" Looking now serious, Marie looked straight at me, "Yes" sitting in our kitchen we prayed, and Marie prayed, and that evening, she started a new journey with Jesus.

This was to be no ordinary journey, and I was under no illusion that she would suddenly become a middle-class churchgoing Christian wearing a neat hat on a Sunday morning. The weeks passed and things were going to test this newfound faith.

Jane was away, family was a long way off and Jane would sometimes make the long journey back to the south to see them. It was late evening, and I was thinking about going to bed when the door burst open. Marie, distraught, with tears running down her face was standing in the doorway. “Nige, I’m in trouble”. Trying my best to be calm we walked into the kitchen, “What’s gone on love?”

“I’m pissed off, my ex has not paid his money for the kids, and I lost it”. “What have you done?”

Marie went on to explain that she was so angry that she went around to her ex-partner’s house to confront him. He wasn’t in and in her anger, she had kicked down the door, gone into the house and smashed the TV. “Marie, that’s bad”. Tears still rolling down she continued to splurge out what had happened. “They’ve called the Bobbies and I’m going to be arrested”. I knew that there was only one thing to do, and she was not going to like it. “Well, you are going to have to go to the station and hand yourself in”, as I thought, this didn’t go down well, “I can’t I’m scared” “Ok, we’ll go together”. I got my coat and keys, and we got into the car to make our way into the town. Most of the short journey was in silence, “It’s going to be ok” I said, not really knowing if that would be true. I parked the car, and we walked into the station. We walked in and approached a staff member sitting quietly behind one of the screens. I prompted Marie to speak, and she explained what had happened. “Take a seat, an officer will see you shortly". We stepped away and took a seat on a bench and waited. We sat in silence; it seemed an age before a uniformed PC came from behind a locked door. "So, it's Marie?" She struggled to speak so I stepped in and explained what had happened. The PC was polite, patient and listened to the account. "Ok, I've heard about this, so let's go and deal with it". Marie stood and the PC placed his hand on her shoulder and led her through the door. He turned, and looked at me, "Thanks, we will get this sorted, but it will be a while, best you get off home".

Watching the two of them disappear, I walked out to my car and made my way home. It was late and I was tired but prayed that Marie would be ok. She had made a big mistake and this could be costly. I drove home and went into the kitchen, I threw my car keys on the side, and something caught my eye. There on the windowsill, were two large false eyelashes, sat neatly side by side, just looking at me. Marie had clearly torn them off while crying, a smile went across my face and I laughed, alone, and out loud. In all the sadness of what was happening I just felt it was going to be ok.

After what was a sleepless night, the morning brought Marie back to the door, "It's done, they have let me go for now". Thankfully the boys had been at their Nan's the night before and were unaware of their mam's escapades. It would be weeks before this event concluded and thankfully after a number of discussions with her ex-partner, no charges were brought, and the event was over.

The whole episode gave me opportunity to speak to Marie about grace, love and more importantly about peace. It was then that she started to see that God was in her life and there were other ways she could deal with situations. Months passed and Marie was baptised and continued her walk with Jesus, a walk she did her way!

Our new closer bond continued, and it would be needed as terrible news was about to come.

I was working in my office at the Foodbank when my phone rang, it was Marie. "Nige, she's gone" her voice was cracked, and she was clearly distraught. "I've just found my sister, she's dead" At this point my heart broke.

Her sister had lived on the estate, just around the corner, she hadn't been seen for two days. Worried, she had gone to her house and climbed through a window, only to find her in her bed. The cries of despair on the phone cut through me, I could hear the pain in Marie's voice and suddenly felt helpless. I had no words to offer and had to listen to the cries of despair, in the pause that followed, I just said, "I'm on my way".

I got into the car and drove home, praying that God would be with Marie and that he would give me the right words to use. Words never came and by the time I reached her she was in a complete state of shock. As I sat in silence, all I could do was sit, words never came. Family began to arrive, and I quietly left. In the days that followed, the funeral arranged, all I could do was listen. I was waiting for Marie to ask the most awkward question, "Why did God let this happen?" She never did; in her own way she had found an inner peace. This terrible time had brought more understanding and the quiet presence of God.

Chapter 20 - Church and Community

Everyday life for the church continued as normal, and for many of the church members, the coming and goings of the breakfast club were only known through stories told over coffee or a short report to the Church Council. Bob and Jilly always made a point of singing the praises of the club, and as other ideas came forward, would always want to add their support.

It became clear to them, and others, that the idea of pulling the church down and making a retreat for a smaller hall was not a good idea. Many in the church had been undecided on the idea and those who had already dreamt of expanding and refurbishing came together. It was then that a plan was made to refurbish the halls and look at new ways of reaching the community. The breakfast club and other community events had sparked imagination and the idea of getting smaller had been dismissed.

With this new determination from the church, we felt we needed to expand what we were doing. There was a real need for this community to have a family friendly environment, offering something for kids and their parents. We felt we needed to separate the traditional Church from the community activities we wanted to bring. Though a separation, we still wanted the church to be at its heart. Through many discussions we decided that we would create a "Family Friendly Centre" and this would be the outreach arm of the church.

During this time, our relationships with families continued, as did our understanding of the various dynamics of this tight knit community.

It was never unusual to have a visit from an angry parent who had been told their child had been in an altercation with someone.

A good example was Terry, who was eight, small for his age but an attitude of an angry pensioner. Games we played were always very competitive, even if we tried our best to keep things light-hearted. Terry would become so angry when he felt his overachieving talents had been overlooked. He was always at the centre of some outburst and always pleading his innocence. He would stand in the middle of the room, arms stretched out, with the palms of his hands held high, "If this isn't sorted, there will be hell on when my mum hears about it". This became his mantra and over time we became less worried about his outbursts and quietly smiled at this passionate little boy. Sadly, we would hear about kids picking on other kids, stories that would change as each parent gave their child's account. This we found, stemmed from home life. If parents didn't get along with their neighbours, the children would be told to stay away from each other. This always proved difficult at the club, and we would often have to have separate teams to keep the rivals apart. On some occasions that didn't work, and a parent would arrive. Jane and I often found ourselves playing mediators in family arguments. We had experienced life with a difficult child, our own mistakes still fresh in our minds. We knew this would be valuable knowledge that we could share, even in a community that was so different from our own upbringing. On many occasions these conversations with parents worked, and they would leave feeling vindicated or sometimes going home with a slightly different version of events. These times helped us to build trust, to listen and get alongside people who had so many other things going on in their lives. We were never overtly evangelistic, we brought, what we hoped, would be a graceful and non-judgemental opinion that would help to calm situations. This approach seemed to work and the number of families sending their kids along continued to grow.

Before long, as we were being asked to do more, we started not only taking kids to school but picking them up too. After-school activities were as important as the breakfast club and many of those who came in the morning were keen to come along after school. It was at these smaller clubs we were able to bring a more Jesus focused time.

Activities always including singing, dancing and craft, all including a theme of love and acceptance. As the groups grew, we had to create different days and Wednesday became Girls, and Thursday for the Boys. The girls loved to dress up and sing, and the boy's construction craft and indoor football. Holidays were always a difficult time, and the need for provision was not confined to our estate. The town was still in great need, and it would be the churches that stepped up to meet it.

Around this time, I had forged strong links with an Anglican initiative, known as "Together". The town was going through an extremely difficult time and poverty was prevalent. Many community groups and churches did indeed come together to bring a new sense of hope through community engagement. Jane and I both knew that any support would be welcomed and with the Methodist Church we could use these links to the benefit of our community.

After a few meetings with other churches, it was felt that we should all work together in our own communities by putting on various holiday clubs. With funding from the Church of England, "Feast of Fun" was born. Each community would run its own holiday clubs and provide a meal for all those attending. As the Foodbank manager, I coordinated the distribution of food around the town. Each club received drinks, snacks and items for sandwiches that could be used during the week. A team of volunteers was sourced for each church, who then held their own themed club. Our theme was "Pirates", and we used the story of Jonah and the whale throughout our five-day club. The highlight of the week was a 70-year-old church member, dressed as a pirate and throwing custard pies. Children came from all over the estate and the last day included a show for the parents. It was a huge success, not only for us, but churches and communities all over the town. The initiative continued and spread in the years that followed.

Messy Church & Community Life

With holiday clubs and other kids' groups going well, we felt it was time to look at different ways to bring our faith into the activities. After some discussion with the church we decided that holding a "Messy Church" could be the answer. Messy church, which involves various themed craft, singing and a bible story, would also bring parents along. We had already brought bible themed activities into our groups and felt the kids and their families could be ready for something else. Getting parents to attend with their kids was not going to be easy but we were hopeful.

We spent a few weeks priming the parents and most, although reluctant, agreed to come.

At 4'oclock one Saturday, once the football was over, we opened the doors of the church and waited. Some keen volunteers from the church had stepped up, and though later would regret their involvement, came along enthusiastically. Various tables with craft were placed around the church. A quiet corner with some reading books was made ready for those less than eager to do some craft. Jilly and Bob agreed to be on kitchen duty and were already in the kitchen preparing fish fingers and chips.

The doors opened and they arrived, they arrived on mass, running through the door, racing to the nearest table. Card and glue going in all directions, anywhere other than where it should have been. The whole space echoed with the sound of kids running, shouting and laughing. Elderly church members trying their best to engage the mob was a sight to see. "Please don't pour that paint on the floor", "Jonny, come away from the fire extinguisher". Jane and I did our best to control the mayhem, but it seemed that all the kids had lost all sense of good behaviour. The break from the madness would come as we gathered the kids together for the story time. Moving to the front of the church we managed to get the kids to sit on the floor. A local children's and family worker had agreed to come along and tell the story. All their training and insight evaporated into the air of total chaos. The kids seemed to vanish in the moment, they laughed, joked, and generally made fun out the exasperated worker who was clearly at their limit of expertise.

The meal would be next, I made my way to the kitchen to see how the food preparation was going. As I approached, the smell of burning increased. Jilly and Bob, red faced and flushed with the heat, were trying to rescue what was once a tray of fish fingers. "I am sure we can make what we have go around". Even Jilly, the calmest of all, was looking lost and perplexed. I smiled, "Ok, I will leave you to it". I walked away, already regretting even thinking this could have been a good idea and made the short walk back into the church and looked across at the unfolding pandemonium. Kids running around, and their parents sat around the side of the church staring at their phones, completely oblivious to what was happening.

As I stood with my head almost in my hand, my eyes caught sight of a young mum sat on her own. She didn't have her phone in her hand, looking intently, she had found a bible on one of the window ledges. As I approached, her eyes caught mine. "What are you reading?" "I'm not sure, it's saying "JOHN". My heart jumped, "Oh that's a great read". She looked at me and returned a smile, "This is quite good, can I, have it?" "Of course, you can". Her eyes returned to the bible, "Thanks, I'll read more tonight".

As I returned to the bedlam, the kids were called for food and the havoc continued. Half an hour passed, fish fingers, left over chips, and tomato sauce all over the floor, and the families finally left. After a longer than usual tidy up, we sat as a group and just looked at each other. The silence said it all and the only thing left to do was laugh. It was then that one of the church members, his face looking angry, spoke up. "Did you give away one of our bibles to that girl?" "Yes" I said, and before I could continue, he became angrier. "Do you know how much those bibles cost?" "I am so sorry but, for me, the madness and mayhem from today were worth it, just for that small moment". Less than happy with my response, he got up and left. Though others soon came to my defence, I felt more disappointment with a church member than I did with the crazy last few hours.

Monday morning arrived and the kids, thankfully less excited, arrived for breakfast. They and their parents praising such a fantastic afternoon. "When are you doing it again?"

"Let's see", I said. On hearing this, Jane almost choked on her coffee as she laughed. What had been a difficult time for us, was a great afternoon for those coming along.

What we had experienced through this afternoon did spur us on to look at other ways we could bring people together. A fun day with bouncy castles, barbecue, and games were organised and the community came out in their droves to join in. Community meals at Christmas and Easter followed. During the week we would hold community cooking courses and other information themed events.

Running the towns Foodbank, had also given me an insight to how various communities were still suffering the economic fallout that was causing a great deal of problems. Though we had a distribution point within the church we wanted to look at other ways we could help.

It was then, through our contacts with the "Together initiative" we contacted a local supermarket who wanted to give away fresh bakery items left over from the day. Each morning, I would drive to the store and load the car with fresh bread, cakes, and other items deemed to be unsaleable but still fresh. My personal favourite was a "Cheese Boule", a crusty bowl-shaped bread that, after being warmed in the oven, was amazing. The food was incredible and the shop it came from was somewhere most people would never enter; it wasn't just food! A large table was placed into the corridor of the church and within minutes the building would be filled with people. No advertising was needed as word soon got out when a delivery arrived. The centre was now being used on daily basis and the community had firmly embraced what we wanted to achieve.

On one such day we had placed the items on the table and set up for a Foodbank session at the same time. Local people would come with their vouchers and collect food. This was always a busy time and often difficult to manage. Sitting at the desk and greeting people, I reached for the mobile phone to make a call. It had vanished, "Has anyone got the phone?" Volunteers looking blank started to look around, it was nowhere to be seen. It was then I realised it must have been taken. Looking around the hall, people drinking coffee and chatting it was clearly not there. I stood at the door and shouted across the room, "Has anyone seen our phone?" Blank faces looked back, and the silence told me it had gone. A young girl approached the desk, "Has someone nicked it?" I wasn't going to make any accusations and decided to keep things calm. "Well, it was on the desk and now it isn't, I smiled. "Some scruffy little…" she continued and was clearly annoyed. She walked off towards the door and disappeared. It must have been ten minutes, and she was back. "Here", and she handed over the phone. "I'm sorry about that, we knew who must have taken it". She looked me in the eyes, still annoyed, "I've told them, you don't nick off our church". I didn't know this girl well and she certainly didn't attend many of our events. Yet, she had felt this building was "her" church and an unwritten rule had been broken. In that moment I had realised that the community had finally accepted the church, barriers had been brought down, and a real sense of togetherness was being affirmed.

As time went by, so the increase of people continued, trips to the seaside were followed by weekends away at a local adventure centre in the Dales. Seeing families getting on a coach, laughing and joining together was a real joy.

The purchase of disco equipment also led to more opportunities, children's parties where dozens of families would come along and hold their celebrations. This also gave me the chance to be the resident DJ, something I always wanted to do! DJ "Ningie Nige" was always on hand to entertain and enjoy the atmosphere of madness that would inevitably arise.

As the refurbishment of the buildings continued, glass replaced the plastic windows, and the centre was becoming a community asset and not a target for abuse. Our dining room table was again a place for us to eat and not the tiny kids club that had started our journey on the Banks. Though our home was always open, the Family Centre was the place that held the community together.

Chapter 21 - A New Methodist

Jane and I prayed, we prayed a lot, life on the estate did not stop because of our church life and we knew God was in charge. Our prayers, as so often, would not be answered in the way we thought.

"Why are we going to a church that is in the town centre, when we have a church here?"

We had made new friends at the church, they were quirky to say the least, and being old fashioned was an understatement. Having said that, it was Rosemary who had started the journey, it was her welcome and invitation that had led us to the door of the Methodist church. This church, just a short walk from our home, in the heart of the estate should be the place we see God work.

We had attended the church for a Good Friday Reflection and had shared some joint services, but the idea of going back to a church with an organ and old hymns didn't fill us with any joy.

Bob was the Steward for the morning, his neatly pressed suit, colourful tie and a big smile greeted us as we arrived. Exchanging a welcome, we took our seats on the back row. Some ladies wore hats, most men wore suits. The quiet and orderly arrival of people, the sound of the organ playing, and the quiet chatter of greetings echoed around the large airy space. As I glanced around the rows of chairs, the odd more casually dressed people started to arrive. Happy grandchildren, brought along to attend the church for "Sunday Club".

As the organ stopped, a smartly dressed lady began to give the weekly notices, flower arranging club on

Wednesday and indoor bowls on Thursday. The preacher of the day was then welcomed, and the service began. As I stood for the first hymn, my heart sank. "What I am doing here, how has it come to this?!" Years of running away from this old fashioned and outdated church, and now I am back!

Old hymn book in hand, I continued to look around at my fellow sisters and brothers and, in that moment, I felt a sense of peace. The voice in my head went back to the day in that old school hall, "I will do the judging". In that moment, I didn't see the suit and tie, the neatly worn hats, I saw people connecting with God. These folks who had faithfully known and served God for generations. I was not here to be entertained, I was here to worship, to thank God, to seek God, and to be with God. I smiled inwardly, knowing I wasn't entirely happy singing a two-hundred-year-old tune, but also knowing God had a sense of humour. As the service continued, we became more relaxed. The customary coffee afterwards allowed for a good chat, and the welcome we received made us feel even more comfortable.

On returning home, I asked Jane how she had felt. "Well, I'm not ecstatic, but I suppose you have to be in it to win it". This would prove to be so true, as it didn't take long before we were being invited to church meetings and given the opportunity to share our vision with the church. We felt we had a clear understanding for where God wanted us to be. In a short time, and in many conversations with members, we discovered a likeminded understanding. We became members and before too long ended up on the Church Council.

Things were getting better and though difficult times were ahead, we knew we were in the right place.

Inside me, I still had a need to serve, and though I was already in some kind of full-time ministry, something inside kept nagging me, telling me, that I needed to do more.

As the centre gained strength, new relationships in the community made, church life continued. The many years before, when I attend a Methodist Church while at school, I had no idea that one day I would be a Methodist myself, hold membership, be on a Church Council, and training to become a Local Preacher.

I had started to feel comfortable in this more traditional setting and valued the way in which the church looked at its vision and handled its daily life. It was very different from our last church, here decisions were collective, a whole church response. This, both Jane and I felt, did not stifle where we believed God was calling us and enabled the mission to grow.

The Methodist Church at its heart, challenged the injustice I saw daily, stood up for the lost, and ensured that each person knew that they were loved and cherished for who they were, whatever their background.

With all this in mind, I still found myself at loggerheads with daily church life. This would often happen when mission clashed with tradition and formality. What had to me, been at the heart of Methodism, seemed to have got lost somewhere.

The church had long been part of the community on the estate but over time had become distant from the very people it was put there for. I recalled that Marie had told me of her disdain and suspicion for the church. "They are snobs and don't really care about us". This clearly wasn't true; they had a heart but had somehow forgotten how to use it.

Jane and I worked hard to break down those barriers and tried to build a bridge between these two groups of very different people.

Problems would arise as we worked alongside the various groups who had used the building prior to our arrival.

As the building was improved, the more it was being used and each group continued to raise disapproval. Now that the halls had been refurbished and the walls repainted, the knocks and scuffs that would inevitably appear were always blamed on the "new groups"

On one occasion, the girl's group had been busy: paint, glue and craft material inevitably had been strewn around the floor. Cleaning up before the imminent arrival of the brownies was always difficult. To avoid the usual accusations of making a mess, Jane spent time mopping the floor to ensure that our prior presence would not be seen.

The following Sunday when the service had ended Jane was sipping her coffee while chatting, her eyes were turned as she heard across the room, "I'm gunning for her". Jane turned to see a group leader looking straight at her. Clearly annoyed, she was telling another church member how fed up she was about the other groups making a mess in "Their Hall". As the two spoke, and spoke loudly enough for Jane to hear, Jane didn't engage in the conversation and instead came to me. Although frustrated, we both felt this was something to be left for another day. It transpired that Jane had mopped the floor at the end of the session and it was still wet when the leader had arrived. This of course led to some annoyance and spilled out at the after-church coffee. We often heard news of the things we did wrong, and they generally involved things that upset the life and normality of the church. A kettle that was only to be used by a local lady's group, a toilet left un-flushed and various other things that would bring condemnation. As the community continued to arrive so did the various notes that would appear around the building. Notes that were on full view of those entering the building for the first time.

Jane and I did our best to follow the rules and though we found this difficult, we managed to navigate the tradition and normality of traditional church life. We didn't always get it right and would often fall foul of an upset church member. A great example was the arrival of a new cooker.

Following the disaster of cooking at the recent messy church, we decided that the old Belling cooker should be replaced with something more substantial. With some new funding we bought a new commercial gas cooker. The larger appliance, with eight rings and a large oven, would be invaluable when we cooked meals for larger numbers. A local resident who was a gas engineer agreed to fit the cooker for free. On a Monday morning, he arrived and connected the cooker. He needed to fit new pipes to the supply, and, after a few hours, the cooker was ready.

The following morning at the end of the breakfast club, shouting was heard coming from the kitchen. "Who the hell has fitted this?

As Jane and I went to see what the fuss was about, we found a church member pointing at the newly fitted pipes. "What the hell is this, you can't put pipes behind the cooker, it dangerous". I was concerned for this elderly man as he was so angry. "The fire chief will close the building if he sees this". He was clearly distraught, and it took a few moments for us to get a chance to speak. This chap was in his late seventies and still got involved in the maintenance of the church. Unknown to us, he did know what he was talking about, and the installation was less than acceptable. The poor man was red in the face with anger, and we were becoming more concerned for him. "I'm sorry, we had it done by a local tradesman, I am sure if we give him a call, he can sort it". Unconvinced, he continued his outburst and stormed out of the kitchen.

Jane and I were left looking at each other in shock, I smiled, "I think we need to get the guy back", "I hope he is ok", Jane said, "He was quite angry"

In a couple of hours, I had contacted the engineer, and he was back, he replaced the pipes in another location and left.

This point, and others were brought to the next council meeting, problems that the "other" groups were causing, and the fact that Sunday attendance had not increased. Thankfully, there were always several people who would be sympathetic to what we were doing and were happy to embrace something new. These concerns never prevented the mission from growing but it did at times make us feel sad, we just had to press on.

I often found myself defending behaviour and justifying what we were trying to do, sometimes this worked and other times it just needed a little more explanation and grace.

Chapter 22 - The Good, the Bad and the Ugly

It didn't take long for the school to see what we were doing, and they became very supportive.

It was a Friday afternoon when I had a call at the foodbank from the Head Teacher. They had a distressed parent who had no food and had ended up in the office, in tears and totally distraught. It was nearing the end of the school day, and the foodbank had already closed. I took some details and agreed to make a delivery to her home.

Mandy was a single parent bringing up two boys on the estate and, like so many others, was finding life difficult. She lived just a short distance from the church and, once I had assembled some food, I phoned Jane and we both went to see her. Houses on the estate were almost identical. Most front gardens were well kept, and it wasn't possible to know what life on the inside was like for the occupants. I drove slowly up the road, passed the rows of terrace houses looking for the number. In the middle of the row was Mandy's house. We unloaded a few bags of food and walked a few steps to her door. The door opened before we knocked, and Mandy greeted us. With tears still in her eyes, she blurted out, "I am so stupid, this is so embarrassing". I had asked Jane to come along for good reason, she was always on hand to give a needed hug and words of encouragement. Jane as always stepped forward and held out her hand, "come on let's get this inside".

Stepping through the door, the smell of cigarettes and something a little stronger hit our nostrils. This was something I had very much become accustomed to while visiting so many people as a debt coach with CAP.

Mandy was tall, jet-black hair, bright blue eyes and her hair cut into a neat bob. When Jane finally got a smile from her, our hearts melted. Her eyes still red from the tears, clearly upset, she shuffled around the kitchen helping Jane. Her two boys, still in their school uniform smiled as we came in, their faces then turned away to the TV they seemed engrossed in, thankfully not too distracted by their mum's grief. "Shall we put the kettle on?", again Jane had a way of being a mum to the mums. "I've nowt, I ran out of tea yesterday" Jane smiled, "Well you have now, come on show me where the mugs are". As I unloaded the food onto the worktop, Jane started to make some tea. "Thank you so much, I can pay you back when I get paid".

I discovered very early on that people would often want to repay kindness. I never challenged this and would always smile and try to affirm.

Mandy was unemployed and, following the breakdown of her relationship, was left bringing up two young boys. As with so many people, life was hard and the respite from the harsh realities were often counteracted with drugs, and in Mandy's case this was cannabis. As we chatted about life, she was clearly agitated and nervous. "I just can't stand this life; I need to work but I've never had a job".

As we talked, her life was unfolding, bit by bit. I learned about her family life, the broken relationships, and the struggle to make ends meet. Surprisingly, Mandy wasn't in debt and had avoided the temptation of using the local loan shark. Money lending was rife, and I had encountered many people who had fallen foul of the quick access to cash. Working with CAP, I would often see the consequences of these transactions.

Mandy was bright but the lack of qualifications or work experience were holding back her best intentions of trying to find work, work that was scarce.

We spent a couple of hours chatting and managed to get the boys signed up to join the breakfast club. "We live just around the corner, why don't you come and see us next week and we can help you". She was clearly relieved by the time we left, and the food would have been a lifeline over the weekend.

There was going to be a great deal of work needed if we were to see some real change and she would need to be ready for that change.

To my surprise, Mandy arrived at our house on Monday afternoon, standing on the doorstep she gave me a smile as I opened the door. "You said you could help me; I need help with a CV, the job centre has done one, but is it ok?"

She was clutching a crumpled piece of A4 paper and was waiving it in front of my face. "Come on in, let's have a look".

Sitting with a cup of tea in the kitchen, we talked through some more about what she wanted to do. Though she had a CV, it was very vague and impersonal. Very quickly, I understood that she had no sense of self-worth. A lifetime of being told she was not capable and not worthy. My mind went back to my hotel days, sitting in my office as the cleaners would come in for a chat, wasting the last hour of their shift.

What I had seen of her home, I knew she was house proud and everything had its place. "What about working in a hotel?" I asked, "I don't care Nige, I'll do anything really".

It was now time to collect the boys from school and we took the short walk together. The more time we spent with this girl the more we liked her and knew that she needed a great deal of support. Her youngest boy joined our after-school club and, as the weeks went by, our friendship grew. She was open and honest and was happy to share her hopes and fears.

Jane and I had been busy all day, the alarm going off at 6am and by 6 o'clock that evening I was ready to collapse in front of the TV. The door knocked frantically, I looked at Jane and frowned. Jane disappeared to open the door, and I heard the excited voice of Mandy getting closer down the hallway to the kitchen. "I've got an interview", what am I gonna do?" I laughed, "You're going to go!" "I'm scared; I've never had one before". By now she was sat on our sofa in the kitchen, excited but clearly worried. Once we had calmed her down it transpired, she had sent her new CV off to a local hotel. Jane had pointed out the vacancy a few days earlier and she had applied. I was over the moon and quietly thanked God for the opportunity. We spent a little time talking over how to approach the interview and agreed we would meet the next day. She was then gone, almost as quickly as she had arrived. Sitting in the kitchen Jane and I just looked at each other, "well that was interesting" Jane just laughed. "I then looked at her, "Did you notice, she never once mentioned the pay?".

In all her excitement and worry, she had not said anything about how much she could earn or the hours she would work. I suddenly realised that though the money would bring a huge difference, she had been seen, she wasn't invisible.

The following day, I met with her and did what coaching I could to help her get through. I knew that if she was herself, she would indeed be seen. Though not full-time, she would be eligible for Tax Credits and would certainly be better off. I agreed to write a character reference, and the rest was down to her.

The day of the interview arrived, and Jane and I were like expectant parents waiting for exam results. There was a great deal of prayer that went on that day.

It was always a joy to see Mandy arriving to collect the boys from the afterschool club, dressed in her uniform, smiling and telling us about the goings on in the hotel.

Life was not transformed overnight, many things were needed to help her, not only to feel more complete but finding ways to cope with daily life that didn't involve smoking weed.

Petty crime was always around us, we knew it was there but if we didn't see it take place, we just had to accept it. It was always more difficult when it came to drugs.

As with many communities, drugs were a blight and for so many, drug use was an escape from the harsh reality of life. It was this that would be visible. The black Land Rover arriving on a Friday afternoon. The scatty young lads handed bags to sell around the estate and in a moment the car gone. Free drugs to distribute, but a large debt to go with it.

The dealers who lived in large houses out of town, drove expensive cars and would never partake in the poison they sold. Occasionally this resulted in an arrest but generally another fast car would appear to take their place.

All we could do to help was to be around those who relied on their delivery. We knew organisations that could help and would often try to signpost people towards them. Those who took the help and moved away often did well, so very sadly, others didn't. Freddie was one such character.

We met Freddie sat on a curb outside the prison. He was slim, twitchy and full of life. We got know him at a Christmas Day meal for the homeless sometime before he would be arrested for another robbery. Following that sentence, we agreed to put him up.

Freddie had a large smile that would fill a room and break the heart of anyone in his presence. He had not lived on the estate, and we thought a change of environment might help him to avoid the influences of his older acquaintances. He eagerly accepted our invitation to stay and was always keen to come along to church and would enthusiastically join in a bible study.

I would often take a walk to the chemist with him to ensure he took his daily dose of Methadone, a large dose that would hopefully prevent the relapse back to heroin. He had spent much of his life in and out of prison for theft, which would pay for his addictions. His life had been dark, and filled with abuse, childhood abuse that I could not begin to explain. He clearly needed expert help, and this was something beyond our experience. Rehab was his only answer but finding places that could help was no easy task. Even in prison, inmates would have to wait months to be enrolled on a program and often they would be released before they could be seen. Prisoners were given Methadone and would become stable on their return to the community. It was, however, often short-lived and they would quickly return to their habit. I was determined that Freddie would not join this revolving door of addiction and Jane, and I worked hard to find him a place in a Christian Rehab.

Having him around the house was fun, he had a great sense of humour and was impeccably tidy. In prison, he told us, "His Pad" was always spotless, bed made, and everything in its place. That was the way he liked it; with almost military precision his little space was maintained.

Over the following weeks, he seemed to settle and agreed to get into a rehab. The opportunity arose at a centre in Northumberland and after a phone interview they agreed to take him. Jane and I were so pleased, and he too seemed up for the opportunity.

We were always happy to leave him at home when we were at one our clubs, and this day was no different.

As we arrived home the front door was ajar, we walked into the kitchen, and he was nowhere to be seen. I walked up the stairs to his room, as always, the bed neatly made but nothing remained. Two days before he was due to go to rehab he had vanished.

Turning out of the room I made my way back to the kitchen and looked at Jane, "He's gone hasn't he", "yes, love, we tried".

We were both so disappointed, but inside we knew that sometimes, however hard we tried, it was never going to be enough. As we sat having a meal later, I had a sudden thought, where is my camera? It was on the side. I got up from the table and began looking around the kitchen. It was nowhere to be seen; I had used it the previous morning to take some pictures at the breakfast club. My stomach churned, my father had given me the camera the year before he had died, and I was devastated it had gone. In that moment, I knew that that he would have taken it.

The weeks went by, and we heard nothing, and we knew we had to put it all down to experience. Jane had become very fond of him and when a phone call came one day, Jane was delighted to hear from him, a phone call from the local prison. He had been arrested while trying to burgle a house and was being held on remand.

He explained that he was due in court and wanted to know if we could go along to support him. We both knew that we couldn't really help him but agreed to attend his hearing.

The day arrived and we made our way into the court. Taking our seats, we soon realised that the sessions were being held on video link and Freddie would not be physically present. The case was read out to the court and the video link flicked into life. There on the big screen was Freddie, his unforgettable smile, and his uncontrollable fidgeting body. He was clearly enjoying the moment and seemed to take the proceedings in his stride. Before the case could be read out, he began jumping up and down in his seat, "Is Nigel and Jane there? "They're supporting me".

The judge was quick to reprimand him and told him to settle down. The judge looked across the room and Jane and I, totally embarrassed, slightly raised our hands. The Judge turned his face back to the screen, "Yes, I am sure you will be able to speak to them at some point, but this has no bearing today". Still smiling, he settled back into his seat and the proceeding continued.

The facts of the case were read out. Apparently, he had broken into a house and was caught trying to take a 75" television out of a window. The problem arose when he realised the window was too small for it to go through. Freddie became animated again, "See, I didn't actually steal anything, cos it wouldn't go through the window". We had always thought he was not the sharpest of burglars and we couldn't help laughing at the thought of this failed theft. The Judge again had to ask him to settle down. After some more discussion the case was adjourned, he waved his goodbyes and the screen was off.

A few weeks later, he was sentenced, and contact came through the odd letter we would receive.

We met him some time later after his release. He apologised for stealing the camera and explained that he had cold feet and couldn't handle the idea of rehab at the time. Again, we managed to get him a place and he agreed to go. He lasted a few weeks before disappearing, it would be years later when we saw his face again. A mugshot appearing in a local paper, a violent street robbery while under the influence. A very long prison sentence would follow, and we would never hear from him again. A life destroyed by drugs and abuse.

Chapter 23 - Pioneers and a New Direction

Years had now passed, and the family friendly centre was becoming more established, new funding found and Jane was now employed. A new minister had taken over from Rosemary and things were about to change again.

There were always struggles with church life and we both knew that the mission we had been called to was always going to be hard. We often found it difficult to fit in and juggling church and community took its toll.

At the same time, I still had this nagging feeling inside me that said I could do more, how that would reveal itself was still a mystery to me. I had come a long way since the time I sat in that seat in a school hall in the south. I was now serving God full time, and yet why didn't I feel complete?

It was while chatting with the new Minister that he suggested what would be a new lifeline, an opportunity to meet other pioneers. Richard was thoughtful and very different from Rosemary, but he too was fully in support of what had been achieved. While meeting one day Richard asked, "Have you heard of Venture FX?" Our response was quick, "no what is it?"

He explained that this initiative was formed by the church to enable and support pioneer ministry. They met regionally and he thought this would be helpful for us. Some emails and phone calls followed, and we arranged to go along to the next meeting.

We had no idea what to expect but knew that we needed to find more support, not just practical or financial but prayerful and insightful support.

With this feeling of desire to do more, we both hoped that meeting others might help us both to see a way forward, and we both prayed for direction.

One Wednesday morning, we got into the car and drove further north to attend our first meeting, both feeling slightly anxious about what was to follow. We arrived at what was once a church but now was a Christian Art Centre. On arriving through the door, we were met with the smell of freshly brewed coffee, and croissants. We immediately felt at ease, Jane and I had always disliked church instant coffee served with traditional brown biscuits! So, it was a joy to be greeted with these fresh and welcoming snacks.

Introductions were made and a morning of discussion continued. We quickly felt at home among this group of rather dodgy and what so many thought were, maverick Christians. As we shared our story and what we were doing, it was such a relief to see faces of recognition. Each person had their own story of how they were bringing the gospel to the lost in new and exciting ways. Suddenly we knew that we were not alone, others too were working for God in many creative and different ways.

It would be at one of these meetings that the inner questions I had about where I should be and what I should do more of, would finally be answered.

We always valued meeting with the group, we had time to learn from others, a time to pray, and space to share some of our frustrations about life and church.

At one of our meetings, we had just arrived, and a face new to us came through the door. "This is Joy, she is a "Deacon". Joy was petite and had a smile that was infectious, and I immediately felt at home chatting to her about life. I had no idea what a Methodist Deacon was or did and Joy was happy to share something about her ministry. As she talked, it didn't take long for my eyes to be opened.

Methodist Deacons were ordained and sent out, sent to be the hands and feet of Jesus in the communities they served. In so many ways, they were just like me, living out a lifetime commitment to serving those on the margins of society. Entwined with this, they were part of a Religious Order, a dispersed group of sisters and brothers who were placed all over the country. They all held that common call to serve, to follow that example that Jesus showed as he washed the feet of his disciples. I was fascinated to hear about their "Rule of Life", this rule wasn't a stick to beat them and say, "You must do this or that". No, this rule enabled them to stay connected, it enabled them to be the best possible disciples they could be to carry out that ministry they had been called to do. In short, though dispersed, they remained close through prayer and a joint understanding of each other.

I was still new to Methodism but knew that I needed to put myself forward for this ministry in the church.

I sat with Jane and talked through how I felt about this call and her initial response sent us both into tears of laughter, "Does that mean we will get a big house!" Laughing aside, we both knew that though this calling was for me, Jane too would be very much part of it. Jane had journeyed alongside me, prayed for me, and had not only been my rock but a rock to so many broken families along the way.

The process was complicated, and I often found myself questioning if this was the right path. Our new superintendent minister was on hand to help me through the process and her care and support pushed me on. I gave up my role at the Foodbank and put down other roles so I could concentrate on this time of testing. I was poked and prodded, questioned and tested some more. Over time, it became more and more evident that this was indeed, the path God wanted me to take. Finally, I would fill the void in my heart that said I should do more, and I would be at peace with myself. It would take two years training at The Queen's Foundation in Birmingham and another two years serving in a church before I fully understood. The need to do more, the need to serve was never going to be fulfilled. That space in my heart, that yearning to do more would never leave me. I now know that it is in that space that God works, prompting me, guiding me, and reminding me of my call to serve. My ordination was not the culmination of a journey but became the start.

Chapter 24 - Closing Thoughts

So, that was the story of how Jane and I took a long rocky road from the South to the North. The journey has been filled with much joy and a great deal of sadness. Yet, in all those joys and sorrows we have seen God working, guiding, calling, loving, and chastising in good measure!

Jane and I recently returned to Oxford to attend a church service; it had been fourteen years since we left. It felt strange to be back, so many years had passed and many had moved on. Yet as we walked through the door, a familiar face greeted us with surprise. Like myself, grey hair had now appeared, but the smile remained the same.

We talked over a coffee, sharing glimpses of what we had done over the years. Our old friend then turned to me and asked, "So, what have you learned over the last 14 years?

The question brought me to an abrupt stop in our conversation, I had no kneejerk answer, and I had to pause. What had I learned?

"Grace", as the word left my lips, I knew that this grace had played a huge part in our journey. This was not something that I had in great abundance, many times quite the contrary. Jane and I have had many difficulties with people who did not recognise our call and would often try to block or change what we were trying to do for God. Certainly, my response was not always grace-filled, and my frustrations would spill over. We have both had to learn how to find that inner grace, that love Jesus has showed us.

There were many times where the church, and us, didn't see eye to eye and inevitably there was fallout and hurt. God is gracious, slow to anger and rich in love, and though, Jane and I have not always mirrored God's example, we have been given opportunities to mend broken relationships. It has been wonderful over the years to meet again with people with whom we disagreed. Those relationships were restored, forgiveness shared, and we moved on in love, not in regret or anger.

At the outset, I wanted to show how learning the language of the world is vital in sharing the good news of Jesus. We had to learn a new language, a cultural language that would help us to speak into the lives of those around us. Two softie southerners turning up to a northern housing estate was never going to be easy. We have learned that we all have shared stories, and though our life experiences may be different, stories really matter. Stories of our faith can have the power to draw people closer to us. We hope that our story of how Jesus changed our lives will continue to bring people closer to us, and more importantly to Jesus.

We learned the language, shared our story and let God do the rest. Of course, we also had to learn the language of church. This language has been the hardest to learn and one we are both still learning.

So much of our journey has been fraught with difficulties, many of those were not always from the people we hoped to reach but from the very church we wanted them to connect to. As someone who had such disdain for the church in the past, I do think I understand what those on the outside of our buildings see. Many churches don't have barbed wire or plastic windows, but they do have so many things that just say, "Please come along and be like us".

We have both learned that traditional more formal Christians connect with God in one way, so do those in a track suit and trainers connect in their way. Both are loved and cherished by God.

The day when I sat in an Olive Grove watching Matt certainly had a huge impact on all that we did on the estate. We had a heart connection with the people, where often it wasn't words but presence that made the difference. Developing that heart connection has now become our mission, not just in our recent past but today and onwards. It is how we do this daily that has led to this story being told.

Sadly, I believe, that many churches have become a world that looks in on itself, they have forgotten and misunderstood the world on the outside of their brick or stone walls. We have forgotten that we, as the people of God, are the church and everything we do or say is seen by those who are yet to know Jesus.

Jane and I have tried, in our own way, to challenge some of the less helpful church cultures we encountered. In their book, Culture Shift, Robert Lewis writes, "*Real transformation is not about working harder at what you are already doing, or copying another church, but about changing the culture at a foundational level*".

I was left with the thought, that if you can't change the curtains, you can't change the culture!"

So, going back to the question I was asked, "What have I learned over the last 14 years?" At this point I need to turn to the Bible, after all, most of what we do and how we can improve, can be found in its pages.

As I started to close this little account, we had the joy of spending a month on the Island of Tenerife. While there, we attended the South Tenerife Christian Fellowship Church. Quite by chance, while getting off a bus, Jane and I looked at a row of shops, and there above was large black sign, "JESUS LOVES YOU, Home of STCF"

We had no idea what to expect but went along on our first Sunday morning. The church was full, and we enjoyed a great time of worship. When it came to the sermon, the pastor announced he was continuing his thoughts on the book of Revelation. Now for those less familiar with the bible, it is not the easiest book to understand and quietly inside I thought I may regret our decision to go in. I was not to be disappointed and following the pastors' words I came to realise that this would be such a blessing and would fit so well into my thoughts as I ended this book.

The second chapter of this book begins with a letter, a letter to a church in Ephesus, now modern Turkey. The letter was commending the people for holding fast to the good news of Jesus. Yet in the praise there came an accusation, "Yet, you have forsaken your first love, turn around and do the things you did first. If not, I will come and remove your lamp stands".

This wasn't just any church, it was incredibly influential in spreading the Gospel far beyond the region. It had been led by some of the most well-known characters of the New Testament, Paul, John and Timothy, all associated with the church. Yet, this church was too focused on "things" and not Jesus.

It suggests to me, that all too often, we get caught up in the theology of church, the workings of church and the organising of church. Budget planning and strategies and so on. We can have great doctrines and rules, fantastic and well-planned services. Yet how easy is it to forget our first love, the love of Jesus that needs to be shared with those who are yet to know him. There is a stark warning within this passage. "I will remove your lampstands". In other words, the light will go. Jesus said, he was the light of the world. The light of Jesus will never go out, but here in these words, it's saying it can be removed from a church. I am left wondering, how many churches have closed their doors over the years, the lights turned off and the building sold? The light continues to shine but the people who pointed to the light have gone.

Having said all this, I love the church, God's people, quite simply because the church belongs to Jesus. So many people have walked with us over the years. Though we have often found ourselves in difficult situations, the prayer and love we have received is a reminder of the unconditional love God has for us. Ministry can be a lonely place, and the sacrifices needed can be overwhelming. Over the years God has brought close friends, they all know who they are, and we thank God for putting them alongside us, even when we were hundreds of miles apart, or sometimes, just down the road. I love the Methodist Church, it's our home, it's our family, and it is where Jesus led us. The open door and the welcome paved the way for both of us to see our potential. The Methodist Diaconal Order, my sisters and brothers are the unseen support that, and along with our amazing God, keeps us going!

Jane and I are broken people, and it's in our brokenness that Jesus stepped in and saved the day! Jesus did indeed bring life in all its fullness. A full life for Jane and me is living in the knowledge that we are not alone; Jesus has walked with us and continues to do so. In the hardest of times, it was this knowledge that spurred us on. Again, the Apostle Paul reminds me:

I'm not saying that I have this all together, that I have it made. But I am well on my way, reaching out for Jesus, who has so wondrously reached out for me. Friends don't get me wrong: By no means do I count myself an expert in all of this, but I've got my eye on the goal, where God is beckoning us onward—to Jesus. I'm off and running, and I'm not turning back. - The Message

To those of you who have read this far and are not part of a church, I hope our story shows that we are not perfect, we make mistakes and are always learning new things. Like any family we can disagree, but love is strong, and the love we receive from God binds us together. God is the greatest father, and though following Jesus can be difficult, the benefits far out way the problems.

What of the North, and the South

Emma grew up, and we are both so proud of her and the Grandchildren we now have. Living in a lovely little house in Wiltshire, she too has now found her place in the world.

In the North, The Family Centre continues to flourish, many new activities take place, and it's not the same place we left behind. Like a plant in the garden, it has matured and grown. A cafe, food pantry, community garden and other groups and services now regularly take place. The church still meets and is still healthy and alive, running alongside the various groups that take place. The lights are on and the light of Jesus shines brightly.

Marie married, bought a new home and though life is often hard, she walks with the Lord, not in the traditional Sunday way, but in her way. We keep in touch, and we still make each other laugh about the sound of farts. She and her husband have often taken the long road to the South to see us.

Mandy, too, is doing well, she works full time, has given up smoking and no longer relies on the weed to help her sleep! She is now confident, and the unseen girl is now truly seen.

Feast for fun inspired the Mustard Seed Programme, which helps people from estates like the Banks to grow in mission and faith. Long after we left, this continues to show how God is still at work. Their phrase" we pray that the edge becomes the new centre" is something Jane and I also pray for, not only for us, but all those serving on the margins of our communities.

We have seen children come of age and had the privilege of being invited back to attend their parties. Just recently we received message from a neighbour's child, now in his twenties. "Jane, thanks for always telling me that Jesus loves me, it's taken a long time, but I now know him too".

This short text reminded me about the time we met a man from another church in the town. He told us of an old lady who had prayed every day for the Banks; she had lived in the house opposite ours. She had prayed that other Christians would come and work for the Lord in the area. That prayer was never answered in her lifetime, and she died before we arrived.

We have no idea how the rest of our seeds will grow; we have been privileged to get a glimpse but only God has the full picture. As the old lady prayed, so do Jane and I.